FREE Test Taking Tips DVD Offer

To help us better serve you, we have developed a Test Taking Tips DVD that we would like to give you for FREE. **This DVD covers world-class test taking tips that you can use to be even more successful when you are taking your test.**

All that we ask is that you email us your feedback about your study guide. Please let us know what you thought about it – whether that is good, bad or indifferent.

To get your **FREE Test Taking Tips DVD**, email freedvd@studyguideteam.com with "FREE DVD" in the subject line and the following information in the body of the email:

    a. The title of your study guide.

    b. Your product rating on a scale of 1-5, with 5 being the highest rating.

    c. Your feedback about the study guide. What did you think of it?

    d. Your full name and shipping address to send your free DVD.

If you have any questions or concerns, please don't hesitate to contact us at freedvd@studyguideteam.com.

Thanks again!

IELTS General Training & Academic Study Guide

IELTS Academic & General Training Prep Team

Table of Contents

Quick Overview

As you draw closer to taking your exam, effective preparation becomes more and more important. Thankfully, you have this study guide to help you get ready. Use this guide to help keep your studying on track and refer to it often.

This study guide contains several key sections that will help you be successful on your exam. The guide contains tips for what you should do the night before and the day of the test. Also included are test-taking tips. Knowing the right information is not always enough. Many well-prepared test takers struggle with exams. These tips will help equip you to accurately read, assess, and answer test questions.

A large part of the guide is devoted to showing you what content to expect on the exam and to helping you better understand that content. Near the end of this guide is a practice test so that you can see how well you have grasped the content. Then, answer explanations are provided so that you can understand why you missed certain questions.

Don't try to cram the night before you take your exam. This is not a wise strategy for a few reasons. First, your retention of the information will be low. Your time would be better used by reviewing information you already know rather than trying to learn a lot of new information. Second, you will likely become stressed as you try to gain a large amount of knowledge in a short amount of time. Third, you will be depriving yourself of sleep. So be sure to go to bed at a reasonable time the night before. Being well-rested helps you focus and remain calm.

Be sure to eat a substantial breakfast the morning of the exam. If you are taking the exam in the afternoon, be sure to have a good lunch as well. Being hungry is distracting and can make it difficult to focus. You have hopefully spent lots of time preparing for the exam. Don't let an empty stomach get in the way of success!

When travelling to the testing center, leave earlier than needed. That way, you have a buffer in case you experience any delays. This will help you remain calm and will keep you from missing your appointment time at the testing center.

Be sure to pace yourself during the exam. Don't try to rush through the exam. There is no need to risk performing poorly on the exam just so you can leave the testing center early. Allow yourself to use all of the allotted time if needed.

Remain positive while taking the exam even if you feel like you are performing poorly. Thinking about the content you should have mastered will not help you perform better on the exam.

Once the exam is complete, take some time to relax. Even if you feel that you need to take the exam again, you will be well served by some down time before you begin studying again. It's often easier to convince yourself to study if you know that it will come with a reward!

Test-Taking Strategies

1. Predicting the Answer

When you feel confident in your preparation for a multiple-choice test, try predicting the answer before reading the answer choices. This is especially useful on questions that test objective factual knowledge or that ask you to fill in a blank. By predicting the answer before reading the available choices, you eliminate the possibility that you will be distracted or led astray by an incorrect answer choice. You will feel more confident in your selection if you read the question, predict the answer, and then find your prediction among the answer choices. After using this strategy, be sure to still read all of the answer choices carefully and completely. If you feel unprepared, you should not attempt to predict the answers. This would be a waste of time and an opportunity for your mind to wander in the wrong direction.

2. Reading the Whole Question

Too often, test takers scan a multiple-choice question, recognize a few familiar words, and immediately jump to the answer choices. Test authors are aware of this common impatience, and they will sometimes prey upon it. For instance, a test author might subtly turn the question into a negative, or he or she might redirect the focus of the question right at the end. The only way to avoid falling into these traps is to read the entirety of the question carefully before reading the answer choices.

3. Looking for Wrong Answers

Long and complicated multiple-choice questions can be intimidating. One way to simplify a difficult multiple-choice question is to eliminate all of the answer choices that are clearly wrong. In most sets of answers, there will be at least one selection that can be dismissed right away. If the test is administered on paper, the test taker could draw a line through it to indicate that it may be ignored; otherwise, the test taker will have to perform this operation mentally or on scratch paper. In either case, once the obviously incorrect answers have been eliminated, the remaining choices may be considered. Sometimes identifying the clearly wrong answers will give the test taker some information about the correct answer. For instance, if one of the remaining answer choices is a direct opposite of one of the eliminated answer choices, it may well be the correct answer. The opposite of obviously wrong is obviously right! Of course, this is not always the case. Some answers are obviously incorrect simply because they are irrelevant to the question being asked. Still, identifying and eliminating some incorrect answer choices is a good way to simplify a multiple-choice question.

4. Don't Overanalyze

Anxious test takers often overanalyze questions. When you are nervous, your brain will often run wild, causing you to make associations and discover clues that don't actually exist. If you feel that this may be a problem for you, do whatever you can to slow down during the test. Try taking a deep breath or counting to ten. As you read and consider the question, restrict yourself to the particular words used by the author. Avoid thought tangents about what the author *really* meant, or what he or she was *trying* to say. The only things that matter on a multiple-choice test are the words that are actually in the question. You must avoid reading too much into a multiple-choice question, or supposing that the writer meant something other than what he or she wrote.

5. No Need for Panic

It is wise to learn as many strategies as possible before taking a multiple-choice test, but it is likely that you will come across a few questions for which you simply don't know the answer. In this situation, avoid panicking. Because most multiple-choice tests include dozens of questions, the relative value of a single wrong answer is small. Moreover, your failure on one question has no effect on your success elsewhere on the test. As much as possible, you should compartmentalize each question on a multiple-choice test. In other words, you should not allow your feelings about one question to affect your success on the others. When you find a question that you either don't understand or don't know how to answer, just take a deep breath and do your best. Read the entire question slowly and carefully. Try rephrasing the question a couple of different ways. Then, read all of the answer choices carefully. After eliminating obviously wrong answers, make a selection and move on to the next question.

6. Confusing Answer Choices

When working on a difficult multiple-choice question, there may be a tendency to focus on the answer choices that are the easiest to understand. Many people, whether consciously or not, gravitate to the answer choices that require the least concentration, knowledge, and memory. This is a mistake. When you come across an answer choice that is confusing, you should give it extra attention. A question might be confusing because you do not know the subject matter to which it refers. If this is the case, don't eliminate the answer before you have affirmatively settled on another. When you come across an answer choice of this type, set it aside as you look at the remaining choices. If you can confidently assert that one of the other choices is correct, you can leave the confusing answer aside. Otherwise, you will need to take a moment to try to better understand the confusing answer choice. Rephrasing is one way to tease out the sense of a confusing answer choice.

7. Your First Instinct

Many people struggle with multiple-choice tests because they overthink the questions. If you have studied sufficiently for the test, you should be prepared to trust your first instinct once you have carefully and completely read the question and all of the answer choices. There is a great deal of research suggesting that the mind can come to the correct conclusion very quickly once it has obtained all of the relevant information. At times, it may seem to you as if your intuition is working faster even than your reasoning mind. This may in fact be true. The knowledge you obtain while studying may be retrieved from your subconscious before you have a chance to work out the associations that support it. Verify your instinct by working out the reasons that it should be trusted.

8. Key Words

Many test takers struggle with multiple-choice questions because they have poor reading comprehension skills. Quickly reading and understanding a multiple-choice question requires a mixture of skill and experience. To help with this, try jotting down a few key words and phrases on a piece of scrap paper. Doing this concentrates the process of reading and forces the mind to weigh the relative importance of the question's parts. In selecting words and phrases to write down, the test taker thinks about the question more deeply and carefully. This is especially true for multiple-choice questions that are preceded by a long prompt.

9. Subtle Negatives

One of the oldest tricks in the multiple-choice test writer's book is to subtly reverse the meaning of a question with a word like *not* or *except*. If you are not paying attention to each word in the question, you can easily be led astray by this trick. For instance, a common question format is, "Which of the following is…?" Obviously, if the question instead is, "Which of the following is not…?," then the answer will be quite different. Even worse, the test makers are aware of the potential for this mistake and will include one answer choice that would be correct if the question were not negated or reversed. A test taker who misses the reversal will find what he or she believes to be a correct answer and will be so confident that he or she will fail to reread the question and discover the original error. The only way to avoid this is to practice a wide variety of multiple-choice questions and to pay close attention to each and every word.

10. Reading Every Answer Choice

It may seem obvious, but you should always read every one of the answer choices! Too many test takers fall into the habit of scanning the question and assuming that they understand the question because they recognize a few key words. From there, they pick the first answer choice that answers the question they believe they have read. Test takers who read all of the answer choices might discover that one of the latter answer choices is actually *more* correct. Moreover, reading all of the answer choices can remind you of facts related to the question that can help you arrive at the correct answer. Sometimes, a misstatement or incorrect detail in one of the latter answer choices will trigger your memory of the subject and will enable you to find the right answer. Failing to read all of the answer choices is like not reading all of the items on a restaurant menu: you might miss out on the perfect choice.

11. Spot the Hedges

One of the keys to success on multiple-choice tests is paying close attention to every word. This is never more true than with words like *almost*, *most*, *some*, and *sometimes*. These words are called "hedges" because they indicate that a statement is not totally true or not true in every place and time. An absolute statement will contain no hedges, but in many subjects, like literature and history, the answers are not always straightforward or absolute. There are always exceptions to the rules in these subjects. For this reason, you should favor those multiple-choice questions that contain hedging language. The presence of qualifying words indicates that the author is taking special care with his or her words, which is certainly important when composing the right answer. After all, there are many ways to be wrong, but there is only one way to be right! For this reason, it is wise to avoid answers that are absolute when taking a multiple-choice test. An absolute answer is one that says things are either all one way or all another. They often include words like *every*, *always*, *best*, and *never*. If you are taking a multiple-choice test in a subject that doesn't lend itself to absolute answers, be on your guard if you see any of these words.

12. Long Answers

In many subject areas, the answers are not simple. As already mentioned, the right answer often requires hedges. Another common feature of the answers to a complex or subjective question are qualifying clauses, which are groups of words that subtly modify the meaning of the sentence. If the question or answer choice describes a rule to which there are exceptions or the subject matter is complicated, ambiguous, or confusing, the correct answer will require many words in order to be expressed clearly and accurately. In essence, you should not be deterred by answer choices that seem excessively long. Oftentimes, the author of the text will not be able to write the correct answer without offering some qualifications and modifications. Your job is to read the answer choices thoroughly and completely and to select the one that most accurately and precisely answers the question.

13. Restating to Understand

Sometimes, a question on a multiple-choice test is difficult not because of what it asks but because of how it is written. If this is the case, restate the question or answer choice in different words. This process serves a couple of important purposes. First, it forces you to concentrate on the core of the question. In order to rephrase the question accurately, you have to understand it well. Rephrasing the question will concentrate your mind on the key words and ideas. Second, it will present the information to your mind in a fresh way. This process may trigger your memory and render some useful scrap of information picked up while studying.

14. True Statements

Sometimes an answer choice will be true in itself, but it does not answer the question. This is one of the main reasons why it is essential to read the question carefully and completely before proceeding to the answer choices. Too often, test takers skip ahead to the answer choices and look for true statements. Having found one of these, they are content to select it without reference to the question above. Obviously, this provides an easy way for test makers to play tricks. The savvy test taker will always read the entire question before turning to the answer choices. Then, having settled on a correct answer choice, he or she will refer to the original question and ensure that the selected answer is relevant. The mistake of choosing a correct-but-irrelevant answer choice is especially common on questions related to specific pieces of objective knowledge, like historical or scientific facts. A prepared test taker will have a wealth of factual knowledge at his or her disposal, and should not be careless in its application.

15. No Patterns

One of the more dangerous ideas that circulates about multiple-choice tests is that the correct answers tend to fall into patterns. These erroneous ideas range from a belief that B and C are the most common right answers, to the idea that an unprepared test-taker should answer "A-B-A-C-A-D-A-B-A." It cannot be emphasized enough that pattern-seeking of this type is exactly the WRONG way to approach a multiple-choice test. To begin with, it is highly unlikely that the test maker will plot the correct answers according to some predetermined pattern. The questions are scrambled and delivered in a random order. Furthermore, even if the test maker was following a pattern in the assignation of correct answers, there is no reason why the test taker would know which pattern he or she was using. Any attempt to discern a pattern in the answer choices is a waste of time and a distraction from the real work of taking the test. A test taker would be much better served by extra preparation before the test than by reliance on a pattern in the answers.

FREE DVD OFFER

Don't forget that doing well on your exam includes both understanding the test content and understanding how to use what you know to do well on the test. We offer a completely FREE Test Taking Tips DVD that covers world class test taking tips that you can use to be even more successful when you are taking your test.

All that we ask is that you email us your feedback about your study guide. To get your **FREE Test Taking Tips DVD**, email freedvd@studyguideteam.com with "FREE DVD" in the subject line and the following information in the body of the email:

- The title of your study guide.
- Your product rating on a scale of 1-5, with 5 being the highest rating.
- Your feedback about the study guide. What did you think of it?
- Your full name and shipping address to send your free DVD.

Introduction to the IELTS

Function of the Test

The International English Language Testing System (IELTS) has served as a standardised test of English-language proficiency for non-native English speakers for around twenty-five years. It is jointly owned by the British Council, IDP: IELTS Australia, and the Cambridge English Learning Assessment and is intended to measure English-language proficiency for people who want to study or work in an English-speaking country or environment. It is intended to treat all "standard" varieties of English as equally valid, including North American, British, Australian, and New Zealand.

The IELTS is offered in two versions. The first is the Academic version, intended for individuals applying for admission to a college, university, or professional registration. The second is the General Training version, intended for individuals emigrating to Australia, Canada, or the United Kingdom, individuals seeking admission to secondary school, or individuals seeking direct employment

The IELTS is very commonly used overseas and particularly in the United Kingdom. However, it is also accepted by over 3,000 institutions in the United States, including almost all colleges that enroll a large number of international students.

Close to three million individuals take the test each year, with the number increasing steadily in recent years. Around 80% of IELTS takers opt for the Academic version of the test, with the rest taking the General Training version.

Test Administration

The IELTS tests are offered in over 1,000 locations including around 50 in the United States. Each test center may offer the exam up to four times per month, for a total of 48 sessions per year. There are no particular restrictions on retaking the IELTS; test takers may reapply as soon as they feel ready to do so, though the testing agency recommends that test takers engage in new study rather than simply taking the test again to achieve a higher score.

Test takers with disabilities or special requirements for taking the exam may receive accommodations by request. Individuals in need of a modified version of the exam must make their request to their test center at least three months in advance. Individuals in need of special arrangements such as additional time musti give the test center at least six weeks notice.

Test Format

Both versions of the IELTS are comprised of four sections: Listening, Speaking, Reading, and Writing. The Listening and Speaking sections are the same on the Academic and General Training tests, but the material in the Reading and Writing sections differs. A summary of the sections follows:

Section	Description	Time
Listening	Test takers hear four recordings of spoken English in varying settings and then answer questions about each conversation.	30 minutes
Speaking	Test takers speak to an examiner, answering questions and addressing subjects verbally.	11-14 minutes
Reading	Test takers read texts and excerpts and then answer questions about the material they read. The section consists of a total of 40 questions.	60 minutes
Writing	Test takers write two separate essays on assigned topics.	60 minutes

Scoring

IELTS scores are reported in nine "bands," ranging from 1 ("non-user," a test taker with no ability to use English aside from a few isolated words) to 9 ("expert user," a test taker with full operational command of English). Each test taker receives a band score in each of the four sections as well as an overall band score consisting of the average of the four section band scores. Each of the four sections is individually scored according to its own criteria, with the Listening and Reading sections scored by a total number of correct answers out of the 40 questions delivered, and the Writing and Speaking sections scored subjectively by examiners according to stated criteria.

Listening

The Listening section of the IELTS™ test lasts 30 minutes and consists of four recordings of native English speakers with a series of ten questions that follow each listening clip. The questions address content in the listening clip in the order in which it was heard. Before the recording begins, test takers are given approximately 30 seconds to skim the questions that pertain to that clip. This is a good opportunity to briefly familiarize oneself with key words to listen for such as places, names, or prices. Test takers are encouraged to take notes while listening and are granted ten additional minutes beyond the 30-minute section window to transfer any answers in the form of notes onto the answer sheet. It should be noted that proper spelling and grammar are expected on the answer sheet; mistakes will be penalized so test takers should exercise care when finalizing their answers.

The first recording is a casual conversation between two speakers about everyday topics encountered in normal social situations. While the topics are similar in the second recording, instead of being a dialogue, it is a monologue—a single person talking about a common life topic such as a description of services offered at the local library or information about a public event. The third recording is another conversation, but this time, there may be up to four speakers and the setting and topic revolve around academics or university matters. Questions are typically more difficult than those pertaining to the first conversation and may also ask test takers to identify speakers' attitudes or opinions. The final recording is another monologue; this time it is likely an academic lecture excerpt or other educational contexts.

There are six task types that test takers will encounter on the IELTS Listening Section. The following list provides the basic details of each type:

- Multiple-choice: there are a couple of multiple-choice question formats on the Listening section. In one type, there is a question followed by three possible answers, A, B, or C, and test takers must select the one best choice. Other questions will be followed by a longer list of possible answers and ask test takers to select more than one choice. Test takers must read the question and directions thoroughly to ensure they properly fulfill the task. Lastly, test takers may be presented with a sentence followed by three possible options to complete the sentence, again, selecting the single best answer. In addition to the variety of multiple-choice forms, the content of these questions runs the gamut from addressing the overall topic or main point of the recording to requiring test takers to identify specific details from the clip.

- Matching: matching questions require test takers to match a numbered list of items from the listening passage or dialogue to a set of options presented on the question and answer sheet. This type of task assesses the test taker's ability to listen for details, follow varied conversations, and correctly understand information or connections between ideas or facts provided via spoken language.

- Plan, map, diagram labeling: these questions ask test takers to complete labels on a plan, map, or diagram such as a building blueprint, a map of campus or town, or a parts diagram of a piece of equipment or science illustration. In most cases, test takers are provided with an answer bank from which they can select the appropriate choices for the given blank labels. This question type assesses the test taker's ability to understand and follow spoken information regarding directions or spatial relationships and translate it into an accurate visual representation.

- Form, note, table, flow-chart, summary completion: these questions require test takers to identify main ideas or facts from the text and fill them into the appropriate blanks in a provided outline. The outline may be of a variety of types such as a form necessitating test takers to fill in names or other details, a set of notes or a table to summarize the relationships between different items or categories, or a flow-chart to represent the steps in a process. Like the labeling questions, test takers are usually provided with word bank from which they can select the appropriate missing words. In some cases, words will be missing from the recording that test takers must deduce and fill in. In these instances, a word limit will be provided, such that test takers can only answer the question with the allocated number of words. Answers that fail to adhere to the word limit will incur a penalty. It should be noted that hyphenated words count as a single word but contractions are invalid responses.

- Sentence completion: these questions typically assess the test taker's ability to understand cause and effect relationships and necessitate completing gaps in a sentence or set of sentences that summarize material from the listening clip. Again, a strict word limit will guide the response.

- Short-answer: in this task, the ability of the test taker to listen for and correctly identify specific details or facts such as locations, times, or prices is assessed. He or she is asked to list two to three points within the allocated word limit. Again, it is crucial for test takers to carefully read the instructions regarding the word limit; failure to adhere to the guidelines will penalize one's score.

It should be noted that not all of the speakers in the audio recordings in the Listening section may speak with native North American English accents. Test takers may encounter English speakers with native accents from the United Kingdom, New Zealand, and Australia.

ETS test administrators model the IELTS™ Listening section exercises after typical classroom lectures, discussions, or common administrative tasks that test takers will encounter in real-world settings long after passing the IELTS™. Lecture topics pull from a variety of academic disciplines in the arts and sciences, such as history, psychology, earth science, economics, and sociology. Some lectures exercises will be delivered by a single speaker, or they may feature several speakers in a classroom discussion format, often between the instructor and a handful of students. For example, the instructor may give a short lecture about architecture and then pause to call on a couple of students to answer questions pertaining to the material just presented, or a student may ask the instructor a clarifying question. After the instructor answers the student's question, he or she may continue with the lecture or segue into an organic conversation that deviates from the original lecture topic but more fully answers the student's question.

The conversations revolve around typical interactions encountered in daily life or around a university setting between a variety of individuals such as coaches, students, secretaries, administrators, and friends. Academic topics may include conversations about registering for classes, purchasing textbooks, asking for directions or locating buildings around campus, meeting a roommate, receiving feedback on an assignment, and asking for academic support, among many others. The daily life topics can include any sort of everyday activity or context such as grocery shopping, visiting a friend, organizing an event, seeing a doctor, or getting a car repaired. The speech in the conversations is meant to sound natural and duplicate that which normally occurs between people, including imperfections and pauses. Characters may stumble over their words or even use the wrong word sometimes; test takers may be asked to point out these errors in the questions that follow the recording.

Test takers are only permitted to play each listening exercise once, although they are encouraged to take notes while they listen, which they can refer to while answering the questions that follow the clip. The provided headset has adjustable volume that test takers can experiment with prior to listening to the scored exercises.

Test takers often find the Listening section daunting, particularly because exercises can only be played once. However, the following are a couple of helpful strategies that successful test takers employ to achieve high scores in this section:

- *Skim:* Test takers are advised to quickly look over the questions prior to listening to get a sense of what to listen for. During the recording, test takers can glance at the next question in line, essentially looking at two questions at once, because questions fall in the order in which they will be delivered in the recording. This will keep the listener one step ahead so he or she hopefully will not miss any answers.

- *Take notes:* Test takers can, and should, take notes while they listen to the recording that they can refer to while answering questions. While it is most important to devote attention towards critical listening, jotting down a few key points or details that seem important can help jog one's memory after the recording is over when the questions are presented. Some questions ask very specific information and this is where careful listening to details and a couple of key notes can be quite helpful. For example, from a conversation between two roommates buying course textbooks at the campus store, test takers may be asked to recall the specific subjects for which one speaker was buying books.

- *Practice:* The importance of practice cannot be overstated. Successful test takers listen to spoken English every chance they get and try to understand the main points, supporting details, and the emotions and attitudes of the speakers. There are a variety of mediums that present listening opportunities from television programs and movies to podcasts and audio books. In-person opportunities include class lectures, conversations with peers and friends, interactions with customer service agents, among others. While formal questions aren't presented after most listening opportunities, candidates can assess their understanding by listening to recordings several times or asking speakers of in-person conversations clarifying questions to verify understanding.

- *Listen for verbal cues:* Listeners can gather clues by appreciating the verbal cues from the recordings. Word emphasis, tone of voice, pauses interjected for effect, and changes in voice inflection can communicate implicit information such as the speaker's emotion (surprise, worry, frustration, etc.) or emphasize that something important is about to happen. Again, understanding these nuances in spoken language will help test takers more fully grasp the meaning of the conversation or lecture in the recordings.

- *Predict:* While difficult, it can be useful to try and predict what the speakers will say by following along in the conversation. It is also possible to try and predict what the questions will ask, based on details in the conversation. For example, if a speaker starts explaining the steps needed to register for classes, it is likely that this will appear in a question, which can signal to the test taker that it's a good idea to start jotting down notes.

- *Guess:* Each question is worth one point and test takers are not penalized for incorrect answers, so it is better to guess than to leave a question unanswered. It is also recommended that test takers skip the questions that they do not know the answers for and simply move on to the next question without dwelling on the information they did not catch. Because the questions will be addressed in order during the recording, if test takers note the clip addressing a later question, they can be assured that they have missed the answer and should move down the list of questions to the next one. At the end of the recording, test takers can quickly circle back and try to fill in any blank responses with an educated guess.

- *Check your work*: Spelling and grammar count, so responses should be checked for errors before the section is up. Even if a test taker is unsure of a spelling, it is better to try and sound the word out and make an educated guess than leave the answer blank. Partial credit is awarded for correct answers that are just misspelled, while no credit is given for blank responses. Entirely wrong answers are not penalized.

Practice Questions

Directions: The Listening section measures your ability to understand conversations and monologues in English. In this test, you will read several conversations and monologues and answer questions after each conversation or lecture. The questions typically ask about the main idea and supporting details. Some questions ask about a speaker's purpose or attitude. Answer the questions based on what is stated or implied by the speakers.

In an actual test, you would be able to take notes while you listened and use your notes to help you answer the questions. Your notes would not be scored. For better practice you can have someone read the following transcript and lecture to you. Also try to not look back at the transcripts as you might do in the Reading section, as this option will not be available on the actual test. The closer you can practice to the real thing the more helpful it will be.

Conversation Transcript

Narrator: Listen to the following conversation between two students and then answer the following questions.

Male student: Hi Deborah, how did you do on the biology exam?

Female student: Pretty well! I got a 96. How about you?

Male student: Wow. I'm jealous. I got a 69. This stuff isn't making sense to me.

Female student: Oh no, I'm sorry to hear that, Greg. I could help you study if you'd like. I usually go to the library after my classes for a couple hours. We could work together on the practice questions and tackle this week's assignment if you want.

Male student: Actually, that would be great. Are you sure you don't mind?

Female student: No, not at all. I have to go to my economics class right now, but I'm usually at the library around 4:00pm. I sit in the back by the reference section. Do you know where the encyclopedias are?

Male student: Uh, to be honest, I've never been to the library here. I don't even know where on campus it is. Is it over by the dining hall on the main quad?

Female student: Oh wow! You've never been?! Where do you study? Yes, it's over next to the administration building on the main quad, directly across from the dining hall. You need to make sure you have your college ID with you to get in.

Male student: I haven't really gotten into a study rhythm yet this semester. That may be part of my problem. I guess I study in my room, when my roommate and I aren't playing video games, that is. I lost my ID at the basketball game last weekend. Do you know where I can get a new one?

Female student: Oh Greg! We need to get you organized. But yes, go to the administration building with another form of picture ID, and you'll need to pay a $15 replacement fee, and fill out a form.

Male student: Does a driver's license work?

Female student: Yes. Do you drive?

Male student: Yes, I have a Honda Civic parked over by my dorm. I go off campus a lot to buy things at the grocery store or to go to the movies.

Female student: That's awesome. I would love to get off campus once in a while and get a breath of "real-world" air, if you know what I mean.

Male student: Yeah, absolutely. Hey, how about I take you with me when I go shopping tomorrow afternoon in exchange for you tutoring me with the biology stuff?

Female student: Sounds perfect! Well, I've got to run to Economics class now. I'll see you at the library at 4:00pm. Let's just meet on the front steps and then we will go in together and find somewhere to work.

Male student: Thanks Deborah! I'll work on getting my ID and finding my biology book...

Questions 1-2: Complete the sentences below.

Write NO MORE THAN TWO WORDS for each answer.

1. Greg looking for help with _____.

2. Greg lost his ID at the _____.

3. The female student studies in the _____ of the library.

4. How does a student replace their campus ID according to Deborah? Mark all that apply.
   a. Go to the library by the encyclopedias
   b. Go to the administration building
   c. Fill out a form and show a picture ID
   d. Pay a replacement fee

5. Read the following statement from the conversation and then answer the question:
Male student: I haven't really gotten into a study rhythm yet this semester. That may be part of my problem. I guess I study in my room, when my roommate and I aren't playing video games, that is.

What does the male student mean when he says he has not really gotten into "a study rhythm yet"?

   a. He has not yet studied with music
   b. He needs to study with video games
   c. He has not yet established a study routine or habit
   d. He only studies in the library after class

6. Why does the female student say: "Well, I've got to run to Economics class now"?
   a. She is preparing to end the conversation
   b. She enjoys running for the school's track team
   c. She is trying to change the topic of conversation
   d. She wants a ride to class because she has to get there quickly

Questions 7-10. Fill out the following diagram by choosing items from the provided box. Write the letter of your choice for each line in questions 7-10.

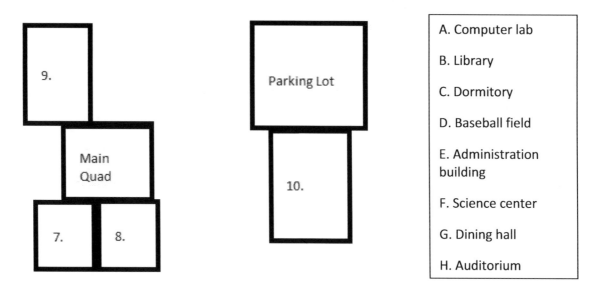

A. Computer lab

B. Library

C. Dormitory

D. Baseball field

E. Administration building

F. Science center

G. Dining hall

H. Auditorium

7._____

8._____

9._____

10._____

Monologue Transcript

Narrator: Listen to the following welcome speech given to community members at the opening of a new arts center.

Female Director: Welcome to the grand opening of the community arts center! We are thrilled that this idea we had in the works for years has finally come to fruition, thanks to the generous funding and support from our town's government, local businesses, and our community members such as yourselves. We truly feel like this center will be a wonderful asset to children and adults alike in our community. As part of our kick-off celebration, we would like to give a brief overview of some of the programs and services offered at the arts center in our first few months, and touch upon where we see ourselves growing over the next year. Please keep in mind that this is *your* center. We are open to feedback, suggestions, and concerns. We want this center to reflect the needs, personalities, interests, and passions of you: our community members.

So, let's see, the mission of our arts center is to promote and encourage creative expression and collaborative involvement in multidisciplinary arts for our community members. This is to be a safe environment to try your hand at new forms of art, or polish your skills on things you may already be seasoned at. We offer classes in drawing, painting, sculpture, metal work, pottery, abstract art, music, dance, theater arts, jewelry making, and paper crafts. We plan to offer stained glass and photography in the coming months. We don't have studios set up for these yet. There are some courses that are offered exclusively to children or adults, but one unique aspect we are excited about are our blended classes of all ages and abilities. We think it will be an enriching experience to allow artists of all ages and stages to share the same work space and classes. These blended classes are held during the weekend. In addition to formal classes that one must register for, there are "open studio" hours every day. For a nominal fee of $10 a month, members can come in and use materials and the studio space at their leisure.

We will take a full tour of the center today, but just to give you a general idea of the layout, we have all visual arts on the first floor. This includes our studios for painting, drawing, sculptures, and pottery. On the second floor, we have music. There is a large room with a piano. We have several soundproof studios for bands to jam together. These rooms are equipped with drum sets, amps, and microphones. We also have a lending library of instruments where patrons can rent instruments for the hour, day, or week. On the third floor, we have our performing arts center. There is an auditorium for plays and rehearsals, a dance studio with a beautiful floor, and a workshop space for making costumes, sets, and production-based stuff. We also have a library on the third floor with books and resources. There is also a snack café and a gift shop where food and art supplies can be purchased.

Lastly, we encourage everyone to sign up for our newsletter. You will receive briefings on the upcoming events and notices about everything going on at the center and be first in line to hear about special offers. Subscribers will also be entered into our rewards program. For every referral that person makes to a new member who signs up for a program, two "arts bucks" will be earned. These can be redeemed for credits for classes, snacks, rental fees, or items in the gift shop. Exciting! On that note, we will begin auditions and rehearsals for our first production, *The Wizard of Oz,* next Saturday! Any questions along the way can always be addressed to any of us here in blue shirts or by calling or emailing the center. Let's enjoy the delicious-looking cake, courtesy of Mylan's Bakery, and start collaborating, creating, and celebrating our artistic talents!

Questions 11-14: Complete the summary below using NO MORE THAN ONE WORD per space.

Community members are encouraged to sign up for the center's 11. _____ to stay informed of the programs and special offers. Members are encouraged to 12. _____ new members and doing so will enter them into a 13. _____ program. "Arts bucks" will be accrued and can be 14. _____ for credits.

Questions 15-20: Match the given room or offering to the floor in which it would be located. Write the letter of the answer choice in the blank provided.

15. Snack café _____

16. Instrument lending library _____

17. Stained glass class _____

18. Photography studio _____

19. Theater rehearsals _____

20. Band practices _____

• Basement
• First floor
• Second floor
• Third floor
• Fourth floor
• Does not exist

Conversation Transcript

Narrator: Listen to the following conversation between a student and the school's financial aid officer.

Female student: Hi. Is this the right place to ask about a problem with my bill?

Male officer: Yes. This is the financial aid office so I can assist you with any tuition and billing questions.

Female student: Great. So, I received my bill for the semester and it says I owe $18,000. I thought I had a scholarship so there's no way I can pay this bill, plus now there's a hold on my account so I can't seem to register for classes and I'm worried they are going to fill up.

Male officer: Ok let's see. Do you have a copy of your bill with you?

Female student: No. I left it in my dorm by accident.

Male officer: No problem. Can I see your student ID? I can pull it up in our system.

Female student: Yes. Here it is. Don't mind the picture. I didn't know I was going to be photographed that day!

Male officer: Oh, don't be silly...you look nice! Ok. Let me just take a look here at your bill and see what's going on. Hmm...Yes, I see the tuition billed to your account is $8,500. Your meal plan and housing in the dorms is $7,000 this semester and there is a technology fee and other posted fees including your parking permit totaling $2,500. The total amount posted to your account is $18,000.

Female student: What about my scholarship?

Male officer: Well, it looks like you have a scholarship that is pending in your account for the amount of tuition, the $8,500. It has not been applied because we are waiting on your financial aid application. Did you fill out the FAFSA? We need a current copy of that on file.

Female student: No. I didn't know I needed to do that.

Male officer: You'll definitely want to get that in as soon as possible. That way we can process your scholarship and also if you qualify for additional financial aid, we can set up a package for you. Some students get additional scholarships based on financial need, or there are loans, and work-study opportunities.

Female student: Oh, that sounds helpful. What is work-study?

Male officer: Work-study refers to campus-based jobs where the compensation for you comes directly off of your bill. There are a variety of available positions for students around campus like in the library, at the sports center, or even in one of the administrative offices.

Female student: Ok cool. Back home I worked as a computer programmer at my mom's software company.

Male officer: Well we have lots of office positions too. So, what you need to do first is register to fill out FASFA on the website. You'll need to put in last year's tax information, so make sure you have that as well. Then, they will evaluate your financial aid package to determine what your needs are. If you want to do a work-study you can apply for a campus job. Lastly, make sure you pay the remaining balance on your account so that you can register for classes.

Female student: Ok thanks. I better get going on this!

21. What is the main problem the student is having?
    a. She does not know which classes to register for
    b. She needs to get a job on campus
    c. Her bill is higher than she predicted
    d. She is looking for financial aid forms

22. Which of the following are ways that students can receive financial assistance with their school bills? Select all that apply.
    a. Scholarships
    b. Loans
    c. Work-study
    d. Tuition

23. When would be the best time for students to speak to a financial aid officer?
    a. At 12:30pm on a Tuesday
    b. Saturday mornings
    c. At 4:15pm on Monday
    d. At 2:00pm on Wednesday

24. Based on the conversation, which job is the student most likely to apply for?
    a. A job at the financial aid office
    b. A job at the computer lab
    c. A job at the sports center
    d. A job at the library

Questions 25-30. The financial aid officer explains to the student what she needs to do to fill out her FASFA, apply for a work-study, and fix the hold on her account. In what order does he list the steps?

#	
25	
26	
27	
28	
29	
30	

A. Register for classes
B. Apply for a campus job
C. Wait for evaluation of financial aid package
D. Pay balance on the account
E. Register to fill out the FAFSA
F. Input prior year's tax information
G. Ask for tuition reduction

Lecture Transcript

Narrator: Listen to part of a lecture from astronomy class and then answer the questions.

Female Professor: We are continuing our discussion today of the history of astronomers from ancient times working up to the present day. So, remember, we are talking about the key contributors that have helped build our understanding of astronomy today. Let's pick up now with Nicolaus Copernicus. Copernicus, in many ways, can be thought of as the first in the modern astronomy scientists because he overturned the geocentric model of the solar system that had stood for over two thousand years, and instead, correctly (but shockingly at the time) suggested that the sun was the center of the solar system and the planets revolved around the sun. This was basically the birth of our present understanding of the solar system – the Heliocentric model. Before we go on, I want to remind you about the geocentric model we talked about last class. Remember, the ancient Greeks believed in a geocentric model of the universe, such that the planets and stars rotated around the central, stationary Earth. But Copernicus recognized that the uh...that the moon rotated around the Earth and that the Earth is just one of several planets revolving around the Sun. He also noted that the Sun is a star, the closest star, and other stars are much further away, that Earth rotates around its axis every day in addition to its yearly revolution, and that closer planets have shorter "years." Pretty important discoveries, huh?

Then we have Tycho Brahe. Now, Brahe was instrumental in determining the positions of fixed stars, unaided by telescopes, which were not yet invented. He made astronomical tools to help with mapping and understanding the "heavens" and the Solar System. He thought the Earth was not moving and that the Sun and Moon revolved around the stationary planet, so we know now that this part was off-base, but he's still a key player in our evolution.

Johannes Kepler was interested in math and astronomy and felt that geometric figures influenced the universe. He built upon Copernicus' heliocentric model and you've probably heard of his three Laws of Planetary Motion. The first law states that planetary orbits are elliptical, not circular, and the Sun is at one of the foci and not the center. The second law says that the planetary speed is faster near the sun and slower when it is more distant. The third law is somewhat similar. This one states that um...that the larger the orbit of a planet, the slower its average velocity.

Next, we have Galileo Galilei. That's a fun name to say. Well, Galileo made many advancements to our thinking and to our ability to make further discoveries, like inventing the telescope. He used it to observe sunspots and discovered that the lunar surface, like Earth, had mountains and valleys. Let's see...he also noted that the Milky Way galaxy had separate stars, he discovered moons around Jupiter, and designed instruments such a compass and this neat little calculating device. These discoveries helped prove the universe was dynamic and changing. Perhaps most importantly, he laid the foundations for scientific thought and process, the importance of logic and reason, and how to do experiments.

Lastly, we will discuss Sir Isaac Newton. Remember, Newton was the one that proposed the three laws of motion that I'm sure you've heard in physics class: an object in motion stays in motion and an object at rest stays at rest unless acted on by an external force, force equals mass times acceleration, and every action has an equal and opposite reaction. He also proposed the Universal Law of Gravitation, which states that gravity is a force and that every object in the Universe is attracted to every other object. The magnitude of this force is directly proportional to the product of the masses of the objects and inversely proportional to the square of the distances between them.

31. What was the main topic addressed in the lecture?
   a. The contributions of various historical astronomers to our understanding of modern astronomy
   b. The importance of the telescope in our understanding of the Universe
   c. The history of how the Universe and Solar System formed billions of years ago
   d. The geocentric model of the Solar System

32. What does the professor imply about the scientists discussed in the lecture?
   a. That only their accurate discoveries or proposals were important to our understanding
   b. That they made a lot of mistakes in their discoveries
   c. That they did not know very much about the Universe
   d. That their contributions, even when inaccurate, helped shape our current understanding

33. Listen again to the sentences about Brahe and then answer the question.
(heard again) He thought the Earth was not moving and that the Sun and Moon revolved around the stationary planet, so we know now that this part was off-base but he's still a key player in our evolution.

What does the professor imply about Brahe in this sentence?

   a. That his ideas were wrong and not important in the discussion of astronomy
   b. That other scientists and other humans continued to evolve from his DNA
   c. That he made a bunch of discoveries we have verified as correct
   d. That he is important in any discussion of the history of astronomy, even if some of his ideas were incorrect

34. Fill in the following sentence using ONE word only.

The information in the lecture was organized in _____ order.

Questions 35-40: Match the astronomical contribution to the astronomer who is credited with the advancement. Write the letter of the astronomer for your answer.

35. He proposed the three laws of motion. _____

36. He said the Sun was a star. _____

37. He invented the telescope. _____

38. He lay the foundation for scientific thought and experimentation. _____

39. He developed the idea that Earth, and the other planets, rotate around the Sun. _____

40. He made astronomical tools to help with mapping the "heavens" and the Solar System. _____

A. Galileo

B. Brahe

C. Copernicus

D. Newton

E. Keppler

Answer Explanations

1. Biology (material): At the beginning of the conversation, listeners should recall that the male student, Greg, was asking the female student, Deborah how she did on the biology exam. Deborah informs Greg that she did well, earning a 96, while Greg responds that he only got a 69. He says, "This stuff isn't making sense to me." *Stuff,* in this case, refers to the biology class material.

2. Basketball game: Greg says, "I lost my ID at the basketball game last weekend. Do you know where I can get a new one?"

3. Reference section: The female student says, "I'm usually at the library around 4:00pm. I sit in the back by the reference section. Do you know where the encyclopedias are?"

4. B, C, D: Deborah says that a student must go to the administration building with their student ID or another form of picture ID, pay a $15 replacement fee, and fill out a form. She mentions the encyclopedia section in the library in an earlier part of the conversation, referring to where she studies.

5. C: When Greg says that he has not really gotten into "a study rhythm yet" he means that he has not yet established a study routine or habit.

6. A: Deborah says, "Well, I've got to run to Economics class now"" to signal that she is preparing to end the conversation. This is a common phrase used in casual conversation to convey that one person needs to leave and move on to the next thing and that he or she wants to end the conversation. She may not literally need to "run" to class, but she is wrapping up the conversation.

7. B: Library

8. E: Administration building

9. G: Dining hall

10. C: Dormitory

11. Newsletter

12. Refer

13. Rewards

14. Redeemed

15. D

16. C

17. F

18. F

19. D

20. C

21. C: The student is having an issue with her bill. It is higher than she predicted. She starts the conversation by saying: "Hi. Is this the right place to ask about a problem with my bill?" Then she later says, "So, I received my bill for the semester and it says I owe $18000. I thought I had a scholarship so there's no way I can pay this bill."

22. A, B & C: The financial aid offer says, "if you qualify for additional financial aid, we can set up a package for you. Some students get additional scholarships based on financial need, or there are loans, and work-study opportunities."

23. D: The financial aid officer tells the student, "The financial aid office is open Monday through Friday 9-4 but we close every day at noon for an hour for lunch." Therefore, all of the other choices would not be a good time to get help at the office because it would be closed.

24. B: The student is most likely to apply for a job at the computer lab. Listeners can select this response based on the student's comment: "Back home I worked as a computer programmer at my mom's software company."

According to the advice from the financial aid officer, the necessary order is the following:

25.	E	Register to fill out the FAFSA
26.	F	Input prior year's tax information
27.	C	Evaluate financial aid package
28.	B	Apply for a campus job
29.	D	Pay balance on the account
30.	A	Register for classes

31. A: This lecture is mainly focused on the contributions of various historical astronomers to our understanding of modern astronomy. While the telescope's importance is mentioned (Choice *B*), this is not the main topic of the lecture. Choice *C* is incorrect because the history of how the Universe and Solar System formed billions of years ago is not mentioned at all. The history of advancements in astronomy is, instead. Lastly, while the geocentric model of the Solar System is briefly discussed, it is not the primary topic in the lecture, as a much more significant portion of the talk is about notable advancements and discoveries, making Choice *D* incorrect.

32. D: The professor implies that the contributions of the discussed scientists, even when inaccurate, helped shape our current understanding of astronomy. Perhaps the best evidence for this argument comes from when she is talking about Brahe's importance, even though some of his ideas were incorrect. "He thought the Earth was not moving and that the Sun and Moon revolved around the stationary planet, so we know now that this part was off-base, *but he's still a key player in our evolution.*"

33. D: The selected statement implies that Brahe is important in any discussion of the history of astronomy, even if some of his ideas were incorrect. Choice *A* is incorrect because she said he *is* still important, Choice *C* is wrong because she is confirming that some of his ideas were incorrect, and Choice *B* is incorrect because "evolution" in this context isn't referring to human evolution or genetics, but the evolution or growth of our understanding of astronomy – how it is has changed over time.

34. Chronological: The professor structures the lecture in chronological order of the scientists' work. Although dates are not provided, listeners can answer this correctly based on what the professor says at the beginning of the lecture: "We are *continuing* our discussion today of the history of astronomers *from ancient times working up to the present day*. So, remember, we are talking about the key contributors that have helped build our understanding of astronomy today."

35. D
36. C
37. A
38. A
39. C
40. B

Reading

The Reading section is one of the two sections that is slightly different between the two versions of the IELTS™. For both tests, the Reading section is 60 minutes and contains three sections with a total of 40 questions. The reading exercises test skills such as identifying the theme, main idea, language usage, or supporting details; understanding logical arguments or the author's opinion, attitude, and purpose; or the ability to draw conclusions, inferences, or relationships among facts and ideas in the texts.

In the Academic test, each text section is one long passage of 2,150-2,750 words taken from various books, newspapers, journals, or magazines. They may be descriptive, factual, argumentative, or analytical and while test takers do not need prior knowledge on the particular subject of a given passage, the text selections are designed to assess the test taker's ability to understand university-level academic texts. Texts may be pulled from any number of subjects such as biology, sociology, business, and literature, but again, test takers do not need prior experience or knowledge of the subject to answer the questions successfully; all necessary information is contained within the passages themselves. The test taker only needs to demonstrate his or her ability to comprehend academic texts, rather than convey an advanced understanding of the specific subject matter. Texts may contain graphic materials such as diagrams, graphs, or illustrations. Glossaries are provided when texts contain technical jargon or specific vocabulary.

For the General Training exam, the texts tend to be less formal and are pulled from materials that one would encounter in everyday life such as books, magazines, newspapers, memos, manuals, advertisements, and company policies. On the General Training exam's Reading test, there are three sections. Section 1, "social survival," contains two or three short texts—often from memos, schedules, advertisements, and notices—that are relevant to basic linguistic survival in English-speaking contexts. There are two texts in Section 2, "workplace survival" that focus on workplace texts like job descriptions, contracts, and employment materials. In Section 3, "general reading," there is one long descriptive or instructional text with a more complex structure, often drawn from daily life texts like newspapers, journals, books, or public notifications.

In both IELTS™ test iterations, the Reading sections will contain the following varied task types:

- *Multiple-choice*: These questions assess a variety of reading skills, ranging from understanding the overall main topic or opinion to grasping the specific details in the text. Some questions may ask test takers to complete the sentence while others are fully stated questions with related answer options. Test takers should carefully read the instructions for each question, as some will involve selecting one correct response, while others require choosing two or more best responses.

- *Identifying information*: Used mostly with factual texts, in this task, test takers are provided with several statements and asked to determine whether the given statements agree with the information provided only in the text and not from any prior knowledge. Test takers are to write "true" if the information was in fact stated in the passage, "false" if the statement contradicts what was presented in the passage, or "not given" if the statement's content was not covered in the text.

- *Identifying writer's views/claims*: As in the "identifying information task," test takers are provided with several statements and asked to determine and write "yes," "no," or "not given" in regard to whether the given statements agree with the views and claims of the text's writer.

- *Matching information*: The texts provided on the exam have lettered paragraphs or sections. In this task, test takers must use this identifying information to locate and pull out specific parts of the text such as a word's meaning, a description, a reason or cause, a comparison, or an effect. The letter denoting the paragraph or section that contains the appropriate information would serve as the letter for the answer. It should be noted that in these tasks, not all paragraphs may be used and one paragraph may contain the answer for multiple questions, in which case the letter ascribed to that section would be used more than once on the answer sheet.

- *Matching headings*: Compared with the "matching information" task (which tends to focus on specific details, language use, or explanations), the "matching headings" task generally assesses one's understanding of the overall theme, topic, main idea, or argument in the passage. In this exercise, a list of headings with lower-case Roman numerals is provided that each refer to the main idea of one of the paragraphs or sections (denoted with alphabetized letters) of the text. Test takers are tasked to match the heading to the correct text sections, while considering that some headings will not be used because there are more headings provided than text sections and some paragraphs may not have an associated heading.

- *Matching features*: This exercise assesses one's ability to recognize relationships and connections between facts or opinions and theories in a passage. It requires skill in skimming to locate information, careful reading for detail, reasoning to understand connections, and logical thinking to accurately link various ideas or thoughts together. The task usually necessitates matching pieces of information or a set of statements or ideas to a list of options from the text identified by letters. The instructions should be read carefully because this task type may take on several different forms. For example, a question may ask test takers to use the information in the passage to match different outcomes from a research study with the different experimental groups in the study but perhaps some of the options for outcomes may apply to more than one group and be used numerous times while others may be red herrings that are not to be used.

- *Matching sentence endings*: Like the multiple-choice questions, these questions address the material in the order in which it appears in the passage and require skill in scanning for specific details. Each question of this type will provide several sentence stems or first clauses, and test takers must use the passage information to match the correct ending from the provided list of options, bearing in mind that not all options will be used as there are more ending choices than sentence stems.

- *Sentence completion*: It is prudent for test takers to take great care when reading the instructions for sentence completion tasks because the question will state a specific word limit that must be strictly followed or the response will be penalized. Test takers must complete the sentence using just the allotted number of words, such as "one word only" or 'no more than three words and a number." As in the Listening section, hyphenated words count as one word, numbers can be spelled out or represented by their figure, and contractions are not to be used. These questions also are presented in the order in which their answers appear in the text.

- *Summary, note, table, flow-chart completion*: Test takers must complete a partial summary, table, or flow-chart that is presented by using information from the text. This question type is used especially frequently with descriptive texts and not only assesses text comprehension and the ability to connect ideas, but also one's understanding language usage and grammar, by sometimes asking for answers to be of specific parts of speech (nouns, adjectives, etc.). There may be sentences to connect in summary form, or boxes and cells to fill in from a table or sequence of events. The content will somehow organize, summarize, or paraphrase part or all of the passage, but more commonly they pull material from a particular section of the text. It is important to note that the correct answers will not necessarily occur in the same order as they appeared in the text. In some cases, a word bank from which test takers should select their answers is provided, while other times, test takers must simply scan the passage and choose the designated number of words or phrases from the passage and use those to fill in the blanks.

- *Diagram label completion*: Test takers are presented with a diagram that relates to a description of something in the text with various blank labels that must be completed with a certain number of words. Diagrams can be of a variety of types, but often are parts of a building, machine, or other descriptive element that can take on a pectoral representation.

- *Short-answer*: Usually these are reserved for factual passages, and require test takers to write a word, phrase, or number answers on their answer sheets.

For either exam, test takers should be prepared to critically analyze the point of view and structure of the passage, as there are often multiple perspectives presented, and typically at least one question per passage addresses the organizational structure of the reading exercise. The information in the following sections should be used to review salient features of different texts and to improve one's reading comprehension and critical analysis skills. While some sections may pertain more to one test version or the other (Academic Test versus the General Training), it is recommended that all test takers review this section in its entirety to optimize success on the Reading section. Following the information in this section, there is a full-length practice test for each of the two exam versions.

Identify Passage Characteristics

Writing can be classified under four passage types: narrative, expository, descriptive (sometimes called technical), and persuasive. Though these types are not mutually exclusive, one form tends to dominate the rest. By recognizing the *type* of passage, a reader gains insight into *how* he or she should read. When reading a narrative intended to entertain, sometimes he or she can read more quickly through the passage if the details are discernible. A technical document, on the other hand, might require a close read, because skimming the passage might cause the reader to miss salient details.

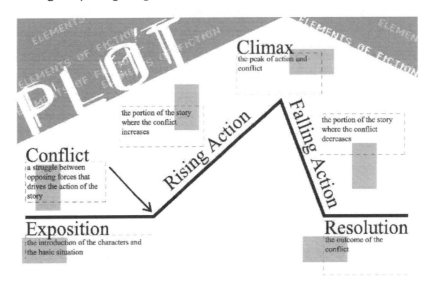

1. Narrative writing, at its core, is the art of storytelling. For a narrative to exist, certain elements must be present. It must have characters. While many characters are human, characters could be defined as anything that thinks, acts, and talks like a human. For example, many recent movies, such as *Lord of the Rings* and *The Chronicles of Narnia*, include animals, fantasy creatures, and even trees that behave like humans. Narratives also must have a plot or sequence of events. Typically, those events follow a standard plot diagram, but recent trends start *in medias res* or in the middle (nearer the climax). In this instance, foreshadowing and flashbacks often fill in plot details. Along with characters and a plot, there must also be conflict. Conflict is usually divided into two types: internal and external. Internal conflict indicates the character is in turmoil. Think of an angel on one shoulder and the devil on the other, arguing it out. Internal conflicts are presented through the character's thoughts. External conflicts are visible. Types of external conflict include person versus person, person versus nature, person versus technology, person versus the supernatural, or a person versus fate.

2. Expository writing is detached and to the point, while other types of writing — persuasive, narrative, and descriptive — are livelier. Since expository writing is designed to instruct or inform, it usually involves directions and steps written in second person ("you" voice) and lacks any persuasive or narrative elements. Sequence words such as *first*, *second*, and *third*, or *in the first place*, *secondly*, and *lastly* are often given to add fluency and cohesion. Common examples of expository writing include instructor's lessons, cookbook recipes, and repair manuals.

3. Due to its empirical nature, technical writing is filled with steps, charts, graphs, data, and statistics. The goal of technical writing is to advance understanding in a field through the scientific method. Experts such as teachers, doctors, or mechanics use words unique to the profession in which they operate. These words, which often incorporate acronyms, are called *jargon*. Technical writing is a type of expository writing, but is not meant to be understood by the general public. Instead, technical writers assume readers have received a formal education in a particular field of study and need no explanation as to what the jargon means. Imagine a doctor trying to understand a diagnostic reading for a car or a mechanic trying to interpret lab results. Only professionals with proper training will fully comprehend the text.

4. Persuasive writing is designed to change opinions and attitudes. The topic, stance, and arguments are found in the thesis, positioned near the end of the introduction. Later supporting paragraphs offer relevant quotations, paraphrases, and summaries from primary or secondary sources, which are then interpreted, analyzed, and evaluated. The goal of persuasive writers is not to stack quotes, but to develop original ideas by using sources as a starting point. Good persuasive writing makes powerful arguments with valid sources and thoughtful analysis. Poor persuasive writing is riddled with bias and logical fallacies. Sometimes, logical and illogical arguments are sandwiched together in the same text. Therefore, readers should display skepticism when reading persuasive arguments.

Non-Fiction

Nonfiction works are best characterized by their subject matter, which must be factual and real, describing true life experiences. The Praxis exam distinguishes between *literary nonfiction*—a form of writing that incorporates literary styles and techniques to create factually-based narratives, also known as *creative fiction*—and informational texts, which will be addressed in the next section. The following is an overview of the more common types of literary non-fiction:

- A *biography* is a work written about a real person (historical or currently living). It involves factual accounts of the person's life, often in a re-telling of those events based on available, researched factual information. The re-telling and dialogue, especially if related within quotes, must be accurate and reflect reliable sources. A biography reflects the time and place in which the person lived, with the goal of creating an understanding of the person and his/her human experience. Examples of well-known biographies include *The Life of Samuel Johnson* by James Boswell and *Steve Jobs* by Walter Isaacson.

- An *autobiography* is a factual account of a person's life written by that person. It may contain some or all of the same elements as a biography, but the author is the subject matter. An autobiography will be told in first person narrative. Examples of well-known autobiographies in literature include *Night* by Elie Wiesel and *Margaret Thatcher: The Autobiography* by Margaret Thatcher.

- A *memoir* is an historical account of a person's life and experiences written by one who has personal, intimate knowledge of the information. The line between memoir, autobiography, and biography is often muddled, but generally speaking, a memoir covers a specific timeline of events as opposed to the other forms of nonfiction. A memoir is less all-encompassing. It is also less formal in tone and tends to focus on the emotional aspect of the presented timeline of events. Some examples of memoirs in literature include *Angela's Ashes* by Frank McCourt and *All Creatures Great and Small* by James Herriot.

- Some forms of *journalism* can fall into the category of literary non-fiction—e.g., *travel writing*, *nature writing*, *sports writing*, the *interview*, and sometimes, the *essay*. Some examples include Elizabeth Kolbert's "The Lost World, in the Annals of Extinction series for *The New Yorker* and Gary Smith's "Ali and His Entourage" for **Sports Illustrated**.

Command of Factual Details

Command of factual details, or the ability to use contextual clues, evidence, and corroborative phrases to support an author's message or intent, is an important part of the IELTS™ Reading section. A test taker's ability to parse out factual information and draw conclusions based on evidence is important to critical reading comprehension. These types of questions may ask test takers to identify stated facts.

They may also require test takers to draw logical conclusions, identify data based on graphs, make inferences, and to generally display analytical thinking skills.

Finding Evidence in a Passage

The basic tenant of reading comprehension is the ability to read and understand text. One way to understand text is to look for information that supports the author's main idea, topic, or position statement. This information may be factual or it may be based on the author's opinion. This section will focus on the test taker's ability to identify factual information, as opposed to opinionated bias. The IELTS™ Reading section will ask test takers to read academic passages containing factual information, and then logically relate those passages by drawing conclusions based on evidence.

In order to identify factual information within one or more text passages, begin by looking for statements of fact. Factual statements can be either true or false. Identifying factual statements as opposed to opinion statements is important in demonstrating full command of evidence in reading. For example, the statement *The temperature outside was unbearably hot* may seem like a fact; however, it's not. While anyone can point to a temperature gauge as factual evidence, the statement itself reflects only an opinion. Some people may find the temperature unbearably hot. Others may find it comfortably warm. Thus, the sentence, *The temperature outside was unbearably hot,* reflects the opinion of the author who found it unbearable. If the text passage followed up the sentence with atmospheric conditions indicating heat indices above 140 degrees Fahrenheit, then the reader knows there is factual information that supports the author's assertion of *unbearably hot.*

In looking for information that can be proven or disproven, it's helpful to scan for dates, numbers, timelines, equations, statistics, and other similar data within any given text passage. These types of indicators will point to proven particulars. For example, the statement, *The temperature outside was unbearably hot on that summer day, July 10, 1913,* most likely indicates factual information, even if the reader is unaware that this is the hottest day on record in the United States. Be careful when reading biased words from an author. Biased words indicate opinion, as opposed to fact.

See the list of biased words below and keep in mind that it's not an inclusive list:

- Good/bad
- Great/greatest
- Better/best/worst
- Amazing
- Terrible/bad/awful
- Beautiful/handsome/ugly
- More/most
- Exciting/dull/boring
- Favorite
- Very
- Probably/should/seem/possibly

Remember, most of what is written is actually opinion or carefully worded information that seems like fact when it isn't. To say, *duplicating DNA results is not cost-effective* sounds like it could be a scientific fact, but it isn't. Factual information can be verified through independent sources.

The simplest type of test question may provide a text passage, then ask the test taker to distinguish the correct factual supporting statement that best answers the corresponding question on the test. However, be aware that most questions may ask the test taker to read more than one text passage and identify which answer best supports an author's topic. While the ability to identify factual information is critical, these types of questions require the test taker to identify chunks of details, and then relate them to one another.

Displaying Analytical Thinking Skills

Analytical thinking involves being able to break down visual information into manageable portions in order to solve complex problems or process difficult concepts. This skill encompasses all aspects of command of evidence in reading comprehension.

A reader can approach analytical thinking in a series of steps. First, when approaching visual material, a reader should identify an author's thought process. Is the line of reasoning clear from the presented passage, or does it require inference and coming to a conclusion independent of the author? Next, a reader should evaluate the author's line of reasoning to determine if the logic is sound. Look for evidentiary clues and cited sources. Do these hold up under the author's argument? Third, look for bias. Bias includes generalized, emotional statements that will not hold up under scrutiny, as they are not based on fact. From there, a reader should ask if the presented evidence is trustworthy. Are the facts cited from reliable sources? Are they current? Is there any new factual information that has come to light since the passage was written that renders the argument useless? Next, a reader should carefully think about information that opposes the author's view. Do the author's arguments guide the reader to identical thoughts, or is there room for sound arguments? Finally, a reader should always be able to identify an author's conclusion and be able to weigh its effectiveness.

The ability to display analytical thinking skills while reading is key in any standardized testing situation. Test takers should be able to critically evaluate the information provided, and then answer questions related to content by using the steps above.

Making Inferences

Simply put, an inference is making an educated guess drawn from evidence, logic, and reasoning. The key to making inferences is identifying clues within a passage, and then using common sense to arrive at a reasonable conclusion. Consider it "reading between the lines."

One way to make an inference is to look for main topics. When doing so, pay particular attention to any titles, headlines, or opening statements made by the author. Topic sentences or repetitive ideas can be clues in gleaning inferred ideas. For example, if a passage contains the phrase *DNA testing, while some consider it infallible, is an inherently flawed technique,* the test taker can infer the rest of the passage will contain information that points to DNA testing's infallibility.

The test taker may be asked to make an inference based on prior knowledge, but may also be asked to make predictions based on new ideas. For example, the test taker may have no prior knowledge of DNA other than its genetic property to replicate. However, if the reader is given passages on the flaws of DNA testing with enough factual evidence, the test taker may arrive at the inferred conclusion that the author does not support the infallibility of DNA testing in all identification cases.

When making inferences, it is important to remember that the critical thinking process involved must be fluid and open to change. While a reader may infer an idea from a main topic, general statement, or other clues, they must be open to receiving new information within a particular passage. New ideas presented by an author may require the test taker to alter an inference. Similarly, when asked questions that require making an inference, it's important to read the entire test passage and all of the answer options. Often, a test taker will need to refine a general inference based on new ideas that may be presented within the test itself.

Reading Strategies

A *reading strategy* is the way a reader interacts with text in order to understand its meaning. It is a skill set that a reader brings to the reading. It employs a reader's ability to use prior knowledge when addressing literature and utilizes a set of methods in order to analyze text. A reading strategy is not simply tackling a text passage as it appears. It involves a more complex system of planning and thought during the reading experience. Current research indicates readers who utilize strategies and a variety of critical reading skills are better thinkers who glean more interpretive information from their reading. Consequently, they are more successful in their overall comprehension.

Pre-reading Strategies

Pre-reading strategies are important, yet often overlooked. Non-critical readers will often begin reading without taking the time to review factors that will help them understand the text. Skipping pre-reading strategies may result in a reader having to re-address a text passage more times than is necessary. Some pre-reading strategies include the following:

- Previewing the text for clues
- Skimming the text for content
- Scanning for unfamiliar words in context
- Formulating questions on sight
- Recognizing needed prior knowledge

Before reading a text passage, a reader can enhance his or her ability to comprehend material by *previewing the text for clues*. This may mean making careful note of any titles, headings, graphics, notes, introductions, important summaries, and conclusions. It can involve a reader making physical notes regarding these elements or highlighting anything he or she thinks is important before reading. Often, a reader will be able to gain information just from these elements alone. Of course, close reading is required in order to fill in the details. A reader needs to be able to ask what he or she is reading about and what a passage is trying to say. The answers to these general questions can often be answered in previewing the text itself.

It's helpful to use pre-reading clues to determine the main idea and organization. First, any titles, sub-headings, chapter headings should be read, and the test taker should make note of the author's credentials if any are listed. It's important to deduce what these clues may indicate as it pertains to the focus of the text and how it's organized.

During pre-reading, readers should also take special note of how text features contribute to the central idea or thesis of the passage. Is there an index? Is there a glossary? What headings, footnotes, or other visuals are included and how do they relate to the details within the passage? Again, this is where any pre-reading notes come in handy, since a test taker should be able to relate supporting details to these textual features.

Next, a reader should *skim* the text for general ideas and content. This technique does not involve close reading; rather, it involves looking for important words within the passage itself. These words may have something to do with the author's theme. They may have to do with structure—for example, words such as *first, next, therefore*, and *last*. Skimming helps a reader understand the overall structure of a passage and, in turn, this helps him or her understand the author's theme or message.

From there, a reader should quickly *scan* the text for any unfamiliar words. When reading a print text, highlighting these words or making other marginal notation is helpful when going back to read text critically. A reader should look at the words surrounding any unfamiliar ones to see what contextual clues unfamiliar words carry. Being able to define unfamiliar terms through contextual meaning is a critical skill in reading comprehension.

A reader should also *formulate any questions* he or she might have before conducting close reading. Questions such as "What is the author trying to tell me?" or "Is the author trying to persuade my thinking?" are important to a reader's ability to engage critically with the text. Questions will focus a reader's attention on what is important in terms of idea and what is supporting detail.

Last, a reader should recognize that author's assume readers bring a *prior knowledge* set to the reading experience. Not all readers have the same experience, but authors seek to communicate with their readers. In turn, readers should strive to interact with the author of a particular passage by asking themselves what the passage demands they know during reading. If a passage is informational in nature, a reader should ask "What do I know about this topic from other experiences I've had or other works I've read?" If a reader can relate to the content, he or she will better understand it.

All of the above pre-reading strategies will help the reader prepare for a closer reading experience. They will engage a reader in active interaction with the text by helping to focus the reader's full attention on the details that he or she will encounter during the next round or two of critical, closer reading.

Strategies During Reading

After pre-reading, a test taker can employ a variety of other reading strategies while conducting one or more closer readings. These strategies include the following:

- Inferring the unspoken/unwritten text
- Clarifying during a close read
- Questioning during a close read
- Organizing the main ideas and supporting details
- Summarizing the text effectively

Inferring the unspoken or unwritten text demands the reader read between the lines in terms of an author's intent or message. The strategy asks that a reader not take everything he or she reads at face value, but instead, he or she will determine what the author is trying to say. A reader's ability to make inference relies on his or her ability to think clearly and logically about what he or she is reading. It does not ask that the reader make wild speculation or guess about the material, but demands he or she be able to come to sound conclusion about the material, given the details provided and those not provided. A reader who can make logical inference from unstated text is achieving successful reading comprehension.

A reader needs to be able to *clarify* what he or she is reading. This strategy demands a reader think about how and what he or she is reading. This thinking should occur during and after the act of reading. For example, a reader may encounter one or more unfamiliar ideas during reading, then be asked to apply thoughts about those unfamiliar concepts after reading when answering test questions.

Questioning during a critical read is closely related to clarifying. A reader must be able to ask questions in general about what he or she is reading and questions regarding the author's supporting ideas. Questioning also involves a reader's ability to self-question. When closely reading a passage, it's not enough to simply try and understand the author. A reader must consider critical thinking questions to ensure he or she is comprehending intent. It's advisable, when conducting a close read, to write out margin notes and questions during the experience. These questions can be addressed later in the thinking process after reading and during the phase where a reader addresses the test questions. A reader who is successful in reading comprehension will iteratively question what he or she reads, search text for clarification, then answer any questions that arise.

A reader should *organize* main ideas and supporting details cognitively as he or she reads, as it will help the reader understand the larger structure at work. The use of quick annotations or marks to indicate what the main idea is and how the details function to support it can be helpful. Understanding the structure of a text passage is sometimes critical to answering questions about an author's approach, theme, messages, and supporting detail. This strategy is most effective when reading informational or nonfiction text. Texts that try to convince readers of a particular idea, that present a theory, or that try to explain difficult concepts are easier to understand when a reader can identify the overarching structure at work.

Post-reading Strategies

After completing a text, a reader should be able to *summarize* the author's theme and supporting details in order to fully understand the passage. Being able to effectively restate the author's message, sub-themes, and pertinent, supporting ideas will help a reader gain an advantage when addressing standardized test questions. Employing all of these strategies will lead to fuller, more insightful reading comprehension.

Use of Print and Digital Reference Materials to Support and Enhance Language Usage

Appropriate Print or Digital Reference Material

Reference materials are indispensable tools for beginners and experts alike. Becoming a competent English communicator doesn't necessarily mean memorizing every single rule about spelling, grammar, or punctuation—it means knowing where and how to find accurate information about the rules of English usage. Students of English have a wide variety of references materials available to them, and, in an increasingly digitized world, more and more of these materials can be found online or as easily-accessible phone applications. Educators should introduce students to different types of reference materials as well as when and how to use them.

Spell Check

Most word processing software programs come equipped with a spell checking feature. Web browsers and personal devices like smartphones and tablets may also have a spell checker enabled. *Spell check* automatically detects misspelled words and suggests alternate spellings. Many writers have come to rely on spell check due to its convenience and ease of use. However, there are some caveats to using spell check—it only checks whether a word is spelled correctly, not if it is used correctly. As discussed above, there are numerous examples of commonly-confused words in English, the misuse of which may not be detected by a spell checker. Many word processing programs do integrate spell checking and grammar checking functions, however. Thus, although running a spell check is an important part of reviewing any piece of writing, it should not be the only step of the review process. Further, spell checkers recommend correctly-spelled words based on an approximation of the misspelled word, so writers need to be somewhat close to the correct spelling in order for spell check to be useful.

Dictionary

Dictionaries are readily available in print, digital formats, and as mobile apps. A dictionary offers a wealth of information to users. First, in the absence of spell checking software, a *dictionary* can be used to identify correct spelling and to determine the word's pronunciation—often written using the International Phonetic Alphabet (IPA). Perhaps the best-known feature of a dictionary is its explanation of a word's meanings as a single word can have multiple definitions. A dictionary organizes these definitions based on their parts of speech and then arranges them from most to least commonly used meanings or from oldest to most modern usage. Many dictionaries also offer information about a word's etymology and usage. With all these functions, then, a dictionary is a basic, essential tool in many situations. Students can turn to a dictionary when they encounter an unfamiliar word or when they see a familiar word used in a new way.

There are many dictionaries to choose from, but perhaps the most highly respected source is the *Oxford English Dictionary* (OED). The OED is a historical dictionary, and as such, all entries include quotes of the word as it has been used throughout history. Users of the OED can get a deeper sense of a word's evolution over time and in different parts of the world. Another standard dictionary in America is *Merriam-Webster*.

Thesaurus

Whereas a dictionary entry lists a word's definitions, a *thesaurus* entry lists a word's *synonyms* and *antonyms*—i.e., words with similar and opposite meanings, respectively. A dictionary can be used to find out what a word means and where it came from, and a thesaurus can be used to understand a word's relationship to other words. A thesaurus can be a powerful vocabulary-building tool. By becoming familiar with synonyms and antonyms, students will be more equipped to use a broad range of vocabulary in their speech and writing. Of course, one thing to be aware of when using a thesaurus is that most words do not have exact synonyms. Rather, there are slight nuances of meaning that can make one word more appropriate than another in a given context. In this case, it is often to the user's advantage to consult a thesaurus side-by-side with a dictionary to confirm any differences in usage between two synonyms. Some digital sources, such as *Dictionary.com*, integrate a dictionary and a thesaurus.

Generally, though, a thesaurus is a useful tool to help writers add variety and precision to their word choice. Consulting a thesaurus can help students elevate their writing to an appropriate academic level by replacing vague or overused words with more expressive or academic ones. Also, word processors often offer a built-in thesaurus, making it easy for writers to look up synonyms and vary word choice as they work.

Glossary

A *glossary* is similar to a dictionary in that it offers an explanation of terms. However, while a dictionary attempts to cover every word in a language, a glossary only focuses on those terms relevant to a specific field. Also, a glossary entry is more likely to offer a longer explanation of a term and its relevance within that field. Glossaries are often found at the back of textbooks or other nonfiction publications in order to explain new or unfamiliar terms to readers. A glossary may also be an entire book on its own that covers all of the essential terms and concepts within a particular profession, field, or other specialized area of knowledge. For learners seeking general definitions of terms from any context, then, a dictionary is an appropriate reference source, but for students of specialized fields, a glossary will usually provide more in-depth information.

Style Manual
Many rules of English usage are standard, but other rules may be more subjective. An example can be seen in the following structures:

1. I went to the store and bought eggs, milk, and bread.
2. I went to the store and bought eggs, milk and bread.

The final comma in a list before *and* or *or* is known as an Oxford comma or serial comma. It is, recommended in some styles, but not in others. To determine the appropriate use of the Oxford comma, writers can consult a style manual.

A *style manual* is a comprehensive collection of guidelines for language use and document formatting. Some fields refer to a common style guide—e.g., the Associated Press or *AP Stylebook*, a standard in American journalism. Individual organizations may rely on their own house style. Regardless, the purpose of a style manual is to ensure uniformity across all documents. Style manuals explain things such as how to format titles, when to write out numbers or use numerals, and how to cite sources. Because there are many different style guides, students should know how and when to consult an appropriate guide. The Chicago Manual of Style is common in the publication of books and academic journals. The Modern Language Association style (MLA) is another commonly used academic style format, while the American Psychological Association style (APA) may be used for scientific publications. Familiarity with using a style guide is particularly important for students who are college bound or pursuing careers in academic or professional writing.

In the examples above, the Oxford comma is recommended by the Chicago Manual of Style, so sentence A would be correct if the writer is using this style. But the comma is not recommended by the *AP Stylebook*, so sentence B would be correct if the writer is using the AP style.

General Grammar and Style References
Any language arts textbook should offer general grammatical and stylistic advice to students, but there are a few well-respected texts that can also be used for reference. *Elements of Style* by William Strunk is regularly assigned to students as a guide on effective written communication, including how to avoid common usage mistakes and how to make the most of parallel structure. *Garner's Modern American Usage* by Bryan Garner is another text that guides students on how to achieve precision and understandability in their writing. Whereas other reference sources discussed above tend to address specific language concerns, these types of texts offer a more holistic approach to cultivating effective language skills.

Electronic Resources
With print texts, it is easy to identify the authors and their credentials, as well as the publisher and their reputation. With electronic resources like websites, though, it can be trickier to assess the reliability of information. Students should be alert when gathering information from the Internet. Understanding the significance of website *domains*—which include identification strings of a site—can help. Website domains ending in *.edu* are educational sites and tend to offer more reliable research in their field. A *.org* ending tends to be used by nonprofit organizations and other community groups, *.com* indicates a privately-owned website, and a *.gov* site is run by the government. Websites affiliated with official organizations, research groups, or institutes of learning are more likely to offer relevant, fact-checked, and reliable information.

Identifying Information from Printed Communications

While expository in nature, memorandums (memos) are designed to convey basic information in a specific and concise message. Memos have a heading, which includes the information *to, from, date,* and *subject,* and a body, which is either in paragraph form or bullet points that detail what was in the subject line.

Though e-mails often replace memos in the modern workplace, printed memos still have a place. For example, if a supervisor wants to relate information, such as a company-wide policy change, to a large group, posting a memo in a staff lounge or other heavily traveled area is an efficient way to do so.

Posted announcements are useful to convey information to a large group of people. Announcements, however, take on a more informal tone than a memo. Common announcement topics include items for sale, services offered, lost pets, or business openings. Since posted announcements are found in public places, like grocery or hardware stores, they include contact information, purpose, meeting times, and prices, as well as pictures, graphics, and colors to attract the reader's eye.

Classified advertisements are another useful medium to convey information to large groups. Consider using classified advertisements when you want to buy and sell items, or look for services. Classified ads are found in newspapers, or online through *Craigslist, eBay,* or similar websites and blogs. While newspapers rely on ads to help fund their publications and often provide only local exposure, online sites provide a statewide or even global platform, thus shipping costs are an important consideration when looking at the cost of the item.

Regardless of the medium, all advertisements offer basic information, such as the item in question, a description, picture, cost, and the seller's contact information. It may also note a willingness to negotiate on the price or offer an option to trade in lieu of a sale. As websites like *Craigslist* and *Buy/Sell/Trade* increase in popularity, more localities offer "safe zones," where purchases and trades are conducted in supervised environments.

Identifying Information in an Index or Table of Contents

An index is an alphabetical listing of topics, such as people, works, or concepts that appear at the end of expository materials like textbooks, cookbooks, and repair manuals. When these key words are used in paragraphs, they sometimes appear in bold writing to indicate their importance and let the reader know that they're found in the index as well.

Index listings often discard articles like *a, an,* and *the.* Additionally, authors will be listed by their last names, not first. Topics may be further divided into subtopics. If you start by looking for the most basic topics first, you can quickly acquire information. For example, when looking for a cookie recipe in a cookbook, first find the word *cookie* in the index and then examine the indented list of cookie-related topics located directly beneath the original heading.

Some textbooks have multiple indexes arranged by different subjects. If, for instance, you're dealing with a weighty literature textbook, you might find one index that lists authors and another devoted to concepts. The lengthier the book, the more likely you are to find this format.

While an index is typically found at the end of a book, a table of contents is found at the beginning to help readers quickly locate information. A table of contents is arranged differently, however, because it provides a chronological listing of each chapter and a corresponding page number. Each entry may also include a description, summary statement, or objective.

When students first receive a textbook, they should take time to preview the table of contents to create a framework for mentally organizing information. By classifying the contents, the reader creates mental schemas and becomes more likely to retain the information longer.

Analyzing Headings and Subheadings

Headings and subheadings are used in writing to organize discussions and allow the reader to find information quickly. Headings show a complete change in thought. Subheadings, which fall below headings, show different aspects of the same topic. For instance, if you saw the title *Government* and the heading *Forms of Government*, you might see the subheadings *Monarchy*, *Oligarchy*, *Democracy*, *Socialism*, and *Totalitarianism*.

As well as providing organization and structure, headings and subheadings also put more white space on a page, which places less strain on the reader's eyes. It's a good idea to skim a document and get familiar with headings and subheadings. Write down the title, headings, and subheadings before you begin reading to provide structure to your notes and thoughts.

Analyzing and Using Text Features

Text features are used to bring clarity or to affect the meaning of it. Bolding, italics, and underlining are all used to make words stand out.

Bolded words are often key concepts and can usually be found in summary statements at the end of chapters and in indexes.

Italics can be used to identify words of another language or to add extra emphasis to a word or phrase. Writers will sometime place words in italics when the word is being referred to as the word itself. Quotation marks or italics can be used for this, as long as there is consistency.

Italics are also used to represent a character's thoughts.

Entering Jessica's room, Jessica's mom stepped over a pile of laundry, a stack of magazines, and a pile of dishes. *My messy daughter*, she thought, shaking her head.

In addition, formatting—such as indentation or bullet points—helps to clearly present content. Writers can come up with their own uses for text features based on what they feel is best. It's important to catch on to the purpose of the text features that the writer uses.

Identifying Information from a Graph

Texts may have graphical representations to help illustrate and visually support assertions made. For example, graphics can be used to express samples or segments of a population or demonstrate growth or decay. Three of the most popular graphical formats include line graphs, bar graphs, and pie charts.

Line graphs rely on a horizontal X axis and a vertical Y axis to establish baseline values. Dots are plotted where the horizontal and vertical axes intersect, and those dots are connected with lines. Compared to bar graphs or pie charts, line graphs are more useful for looking at the past and present and predicting future outcomes. For instance, a potential investor would look for stocks that demonstrated steady growth over many decades when examining the stock market. Note that severe spikes up and down indicate instability, while line graphs that display a slow but steady increase may indicate good returns.

Here's an example of a bar graph:

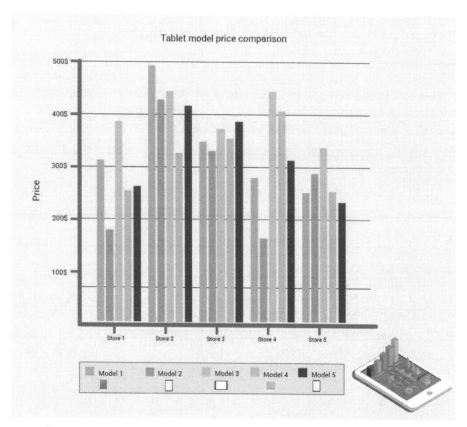

Bar graphs are usually displayed on a vertical Y axis. The bars themselves can be two- or three-dimensional, depending on the designer's tastes. Unlike a line graph, which shows the fluctuation of only one variable, the X axis on a bar graph is excellent for making comparisons, because it shows differences between several variables. For instance, if a consumer wanted to buy a new tablet, she could narrow the selection down to a few choices by using a bar graph to plot the prices side by side. The tallest bar would be the most expensive tablet, the shortest bar would be the cheapest.

A pie chart is divided into wedges that represent a numerical piece of the whole. Pie charts are useful for demonstrating how different categories add up to 100 percent. However, pie charts are not useful in comparing dissimilar items. High schools tend to use pie charts to track where students end up after graduation. Each wedge, for instance, might be labeled *vocational school, two-year college, four-year college, workforce,* or *unemployed.* By calculating the size of each wedge, schools can offer classes in the same ratios as where students will end up after high school. Pie charts are also useful for tracking finances. Items like car payments, insurance, rent, credit cards, and entertainment would each get their own wedge proportional to the amount spent in a given time period. If one wedge is inordinately bigger than the rest, or if a wedge is expendable, it might be time to create a new financial strategy.

Identifying Scale Readings

Most measuring instruments have scales to allow someone to determine precise measurement. Many of these instruments are becoming digitized such that the screens output measurement; for example, weighing scales and tire-pressure gauges often have digital screens. However, it's still important to know how to read scales. Many rulers have scales for inches on one side and scales for centimeters on the other side. On the inches' side, the longest black lines indicate the inch marks, and the slightly shorter lines indicate the half-inch marks. Progressively shorter black lines indicate the quarter-inch, eighth-inch, and sometimes even sixteenth-inch marks.

Using Legends and Map Keys

Legends and map keys are placed on maps to identify what the symbols on the map represent. Generally, map symbols stand for things like railroads, national or state highways, and public parks. Legends and maps keys can generally be found in the bottom right corner of a map. They are necessary to avoid the needless repetition of the same information because of the large amounts of information condensed onto a map. In addition, there may be a compass rose that shows the directions of north, south, east, and west. Most maps are oriented such that the top of the map is north.

Maps also have scales, which are a type of legend or key that show relative distances between fixed points. If you were on a highway and nearly out of gas, a map's scale would help you determine if you could make it to the next town before running out of fuel.

Evaluating Product Information to Determine the most Economical Buy

When evaluating product information, be on the lookout for bolded and italicized words and numbers, which indicate the information is especially important. Also be on the lookout for repeated or similar information, which indicates importance. If you're trying to find the best deal, it might be useful to do a side-by-side comparison. Using software, like Microsoft Excel, can help you organize and compare costs systematically.

In addition, being a savvy shopper in today's market means not only having a decent grasp of math, but also understanding how retailers use established techniques to encourage consumers to spend more. Look for units of measurement—pounds, ounces, liters, grams, etc.—then divide the amount by the cost. By comparing this way, you may find products on sale cost more than ones that are not.

You should also take into consideration any tax or shipping costs. Obviously, the more an item costs, the more tax or shipping tends to cost too. Most brick and mortar establishments, like Target, Walmart, and Sears, are required to charge tax based on location, but some internet sites, like Amazon, Overstock, and eBay, will offer no tax or free shipping as an incentive. Comparisons between local stores and internet sites can aid in finding the best deal.

Identifying Information from a Telephone Book

The yellow pages in printed telephone books offer an alphabetical listing of businesses and services. Along with basic contact information—address, phone number, and business information—some will pay more to include an advertisement. Though more flashy and engaging than basic contact information, ads are not necessarily indicative of better service. Similar to the yellow pages, the white pages offer an alphabetical listing of people's names, addresses, and phone numbers. The blue pages provide an alphabetical listing of government agencies and numbers. Most of the information previously only available in telephone books can now be found online.

Identifying Information from a Listing of Items

When similar items are sold, they are often placed in tables or charts for the consumer's convenience. Either scanning horizontally across a row or vertically down a column (or a combination of both) provides the opportunity for a quick comparison. Basic math plays a part in the decision making, but consumers should also consider warranties, product reputations, and hidden costs, such as tax or shipping.

For example, consider menus. Meals are individually labeled or multiple items are grouped under one heading, such as appetizers or main dishes. Substitutions may or may not have an added cost. Drinks might be ordered separately or included with the meal. Some restaurants offer free refills while others charge for each glass. If in doubt, ask your server. Regardless of the order, sales tax or a tip is seldom included. If gratuity is included, it's usually due to the size of your party and is noted on the menu. A 15-20 percent tip is customary in the United States.

For movie listings, however, prices may fluctuate based on age (teenager versus senior citizen) and time (early-bird showing versus evening). Movie listings are typically oriented vertically, either on a marquis, a display, or an easel. The current movies are usually listed with each of their show times.

Here's an example of information you could get from a menu:

Main Idea

It is very important to know the difference between the topic and the main idea of the text. Even though these two are similar because they both present the central point of a text, they have distinctive differences. A *topic* is the subject of the text; it can usually be described in a one- to two-word phrase and appears in the simplest form. On the other hand, the *main idea* is more detailed and provides the author's central point of the text. It can be expressed through a complete sentence and can be found in the beginning, middle, or end of a paragraph. In most nonfiction books, the first sentence of the passage usually (but not always) states the main idea. Take a look at the passage below to review the topic versus the main idea.

Cheetahs

Cheetahs are one of the fastest mammals on land, reaching up to 70 miles an hour over short distances. Even though cheetahs can run as fast as 70 miles an hour, they usually only have to run half that speed to catch up with their choice of prey. Cheetahs cannot maintain a fast pace over long periods of time because they will overheat their bodies. After a chase, cheetahs need to rest for approximately 30 minutes prior to eating or returning to any other activity.

In the example above, the topic of the passage is "Cheetahs" simply because that is the subject of the text. The main idea of the text is "Cheetahs are one of the fastest mammals on land but can only maintain this fast pace for short distances." While it covers the topic, it is more detailed and refers to the text in its entirety. The text continues to provide additional details called *supporting details,* which will be discussed in the next section.

SupportiG1769ng Details

Supporting details help readers better develop and understand the main idea. Supporting details answer questions like *who, what, where, when, why,* and *how.* Different types of supporting details include examples, facts and statistics, anecdotes, and sensory details.

Persuasive and informative texts often use supporting details. In persuasive texts, authors attempt to make readers agree with their point of view, and supporting details are often used as "selling points." If authors make a statement, they should support the statement with evidence in order to adequately persuade readers. Informative texts use supporting details such as examples and facts to inform readers. Take another look at the previous "Cheetahs" passage to find examples of supporting details.

Cheetahs

Cheetahs are one of the fastest mammals on land, reaching up to 70 miles an hour over short distances. Even though cheetahs can run as fast as 70 miles an hour, they usually only have to run half that speed to catch up with their choice of prey. Cheetahs cannot maintain a fast pace over long periods of time because they will overheat their bodies. After a chase, cheetahs need to rest for approximately 30 minutes prior to eating or returning to any other activity.

In the example above, supporting details include:

- Cheetahs reach up to 70 miles per hour over short distances.
- They usually only have to run half that speed to catch up with their prey.
- Cheetahs will overheat their bodies if they exert a high speed over longer distances.
- Cheetahs need to rest for 30 minutes after a chase.

Look at the diagram below (applying the cheetah example) to help determine the hierarchy of topic, main idea, and supporting details.

Vocabulary

Vocabulary

Vocabulary consists of the bank of words that readers can understand and apply fluently in order to communicate effectively. A strong vocabulary and word recognition base enables readers to access prior knowledge and experiences in order to make connections in written texts. A strong vocabulary also allows readers to express ideas, learn new concepts, and decode the meanings of unfamiliar words by using context clues. Conversely, if a reader's vocabulary knowledge is limited and does not steadily increase, reading comprehension will be negatively affected. English language learners who have a limited vocabulary can become frustrated with their lack of understanding of written texts, and may be inclined to choose to only read texts at their comfort level or refuse to read altogether. There are a variety of strategies that can be employed to improve vocabulary, which will enhance reading comprehension, including learning about the roots of words, the structure of text, and exposing oneself to a variety of written and oral language experiences.

Morphology

The study of morphology generally deals with the structure and formation of words. A phoneme is the smallest unit of sound that does not necessarily carry meaning. Essentially, phonemes are combined to form words, and words are combined to form sentences. Morphology looks at the smallest meaningful part of a word, known as a morpheme. In contrast to a phoneme, a morpheme must carry a sound and a meaning. Free morphemes are those that can stand alone, carrying both sound and meaning, as in the following words: girl, boy, man, and lady. Just as the name suggests, bound morphemes are bound to other morphemes in order to carry meaning. Examples of bound morphemes include: ish, ness, ly, and dis.

Semantics

Semantics is the branch of linguistics that addresses meanings. Morphemes, words, phrases, and sentences all carry distinct meanings. The way these individual parts are arranged can have a significant effect on meaning. In order to construct language, readers must be able to use semantics to arrange and rearrange words to achieve the particular meaning they are striving for. Activities that improve on'e understanding of semantics revolve around studying the arrangement of word parts (morphology) and root words, and then the studying vocabulary. Moving from vocabulary words into studying sentences and sentence structure leads readers to learn how to use context clues to determine meaning and to understand anomalies such as metaphors, idioms, and allusions. There are five types of semantic relationships that are critical to understand:

Hyponyms refer to a relationship between words where general words have multiple more-specific words (hyponyms) that fall into the same category (e.g., horse: mare, stallion, foal, Appaloosa, Clydesdale).

Meronyms refer to a relationship between words where a whole word has multiple parts (meronyms) that comprise it (e.g., horse: tail, mane, hooves, ears).

Synonyms refer to words that have the same meaning as another word (e.g., instructor/teacher/educator, canine/dog, feline/cat, herbivore/vegetarian).

Antonyms refer to words that have the opposite meaning as another word (e.g., true/false, up/down, in/out, right/wrong).

Homonyms refer to words that are spelled the same (homographs) or sound the same (homophones) but mean different things (e.g., there/their/they're, two/too/to, principal/principle, plain/plane, (kitchen) sink/ sink (down as in water)).

Understanding the Use of Affixes, Context, and Syntax

<u>Affixes</u>

Individual words are constructed from building blocks of meaning. An *affix* is an element that is added to a root or stem word that can change the word's meaning.

For example, the stem word *fix* is a verb meaning *to repair*. When the ending *–able* is added, it becomes the adjective *fixable*, meaning "capable of being repaired." Adding *un–* to the beginning changes the word to *unfixable*, meaning "incapable of being repaired." In this way, affixes attach to the word stem to create a new word and a new meaning. Knowledge of affixes can assist in deciphering the meaning of unfamiliar words.

Affixes are also related to inflection. *Inflection* is the modification of a base word to express a different grammatical or syntactical function. For example, countable nouns such as *car* and *airport* become plural with the addition of *–s* at the end: *cars* and *airports*.

Verb tense is also expressed through inflection. *Regular verbs*—those that follow a standard inflection pattern—can be changed to past tense using the affixes *–ed, –d,* or *–ied*, as in *cooked* and *studied*. Verbs can also be modified for continuous tenses by using *–ing*, as in *working* or *exploring*. Thus, affixes are used not only to express meaning but also to reflect a word's grammatical purpose.

A *prefix* is an affix attached to the beginning of a word. The meanings of English prefixes mainly come from Greek and Latin origins. The chart below contains a few of the most commonly used English prefixes.

Prefix	Meaning	Example
a-	Not	amoral, asymptomatic
anti-	Against	antidote, antifreeze
auto-	Self	automobile, automatic
circum-	Around	circumference, circumspect
co-, com-, con-	Together	coworker, companion
contra-	Against	contradict, contrary
de-	negation or reversal	deflate, deodorant
extra-	outside, beyond	extraterrestrial, extracurricular
in-, im-, il-, ir-	Not	impossible, irregular
inter-	Between	international, intervene
intra-	Within	intramural, intranet
mis-	Wrongly	mistake, misunderstand
mono-	One	monolith, monopoly
non-	Not	nonpartisan, nonsense
pre-	Before	preview, prediction
re-	Again	review, renew
semi-	Half	semicircle, semicolon
sub-	Under	subway, submarine
super-	Above	superhuman, superintendent
trans-	across, beyond, through	trans-Siberian, transform
un-	Not	unwelcome, unfriendly

While the addition of a prefix alters the meaning of the base word, the addition of a *suffix* may also affect a word's part of speech. For example, adding a suffix can change the noun *material* into the verb *materialize* and back to a noun again in *materialization*.

Suffix	Part of Speech	Meaning	Example
-able, -ible	adjective	having the ability to	honorable, flexible
-acy, -cy	noun	state or quality	intimacy, dependency
-al, -ical	adjective	having the quality of	historical, tribal
-en	verb	to cause to become	strengthen, embolden
-er, -ier	adjective	comparative	happier, longer
-est, -iest	adjective	superlative	sunniest, hottest
-ess	noun	female	waitress, actress
-ful	adjective	full of, characterized by	beautiful, thankful
-fy, -ify	verb	to cause, to come to be	liquefy, intensify
-ism	noun	doctrine, belief, action	Communism, Buddhism
-ive, -ative, -itive	adjective	having the quality of	creative, innovative
-ize	verb	to convert into, to subject to	Americanize, dramatize
-less	adjective	without, missing	emotionless, hopeless
-ly	adverb	in the manner of	quickly, energetically
-ness	noun	quality or state	goodness, darkness
-ous, -ious, -eous	adjective	having the quality of	spontaneous, pious
-ship	noun	status or condition	partnership, ownership
-tion	noun	action or state	renovation, promotion
-y	adjective	characterized by	smoky, dreamy

Through knowledge of prefixes and suffixes, a student's vocabulary can be instantly expanded with an understanding of *etymology*—the origin of words. This, in turn, can be used to add sentence structure variety to academic writing.

Context Clues

Familiarity with common prefixes, suffixes, and root words assists tremendously in unraveling the meaning of an unfamiliar word and making an educated guess as to its meaning. However, some words do not contain many easily-identifiable clues that point to their meaning. In this case, rather than looking at the elements within the word, it is useful to consider elements around the word—i.e., its context. *Context* refers to the other words and information within the sentence or surrounding sentences that indicate the unknown word's probable meaning. The following sentences provide context for the potentially-unfamiliar word *quixotic*:

> Rebecca had never been one to settle into a predictable, ordinary life. Her quixotic personality led her to leave behind a job with a prestigious law firm in Manhattan and move halfway around the world to pursue her dream of becoming a sushi chef in Tokyo.

A reader unfamiliar with the word *quixotic* doesn't have many clues to use in terms of affixes or root meaning. The suffix *–ic* indicates that the word is an adjective, but that is it. In this case, then, a reader would need to look at surrounding information to obtain some clues about the word. Other adjectives in the passage include *predictable* and *ordinary*, things that Rebecca was definitely not, as indicated by

"Rebecca had never been one to settle." Thus, a first clue might be that *quixotic* means the opposite of predictable.

The second sentence doesn't offer any other modifier of *personality* other than *quixotic*, but it does include a story that reveals further information about her personality. She had a stable, respectable job, but she decided to give it up to follow her dream. Combining these two ideas together, then— unpredictable and dream-seeking—gives the reader a general idea of what *quixotic* probably means. In fact, the root of the word is the character Don Quixote, a romantic dreamer who goes on an impulsive adventure.

While context clues are useful for making an approximate definition for newly-encountered words, these types of clues also come in handy when encountering common words that have multiple meanings. The word *reservation* is used differently in each the following sentences:

- That restaurant is booked solid for the next month; it's impossible to make a reservation unless you know somebody.

- The hospital plans to open a branch office inside the reservation to better serve Native American patients who cannot easily travel to the main hospital fifty miles away.

- Janet Clark is a dependable, knowledgeable worker, and I recommend her for the position of team leader without reservation.

All three sentences use the word to express different meanings. In fact, most words in English have more than one meaning—sometimes meanings that are completely different from one another. Thus, context can provide clues as to which meaning is appropriate in a given situation. A quick search in the dictionary reveals several possible meanings for *reservation*:

1. An exception or qualification
2. A tract of public land set aside, such as for the use of American Indian tribes
3. An arrangement for accommodations, such as in a hotel, on a plane, or at a restaurant

Sentence A mentions a restaurant, making the third definition the correct one in this case. In sentence B, some context clues include Native Americans, as well as the implication that a reservation is a place— "inside the reservation," both of which indicate that the second definition should be used here. Finally, sentence C uses *without reservation* to mean "completely" or "without exception," so the first definition can be applied here.

Using context clues in this way can be especially useful for words that have multiple, widely varying meanings. If a word has more than one definition and two of those definitions are the opposite of each other, it is known as an *auto-antonym*—a word that can also be its own antonym. In the case of auto-antonyms, context clues are crucial to determine which definition to employ in a given sentence. For example, the word *sanction* can either mean "to approve or allow" or "a penalty." Approving and penalizing have opposite meanings, so *sanction* is an example of an auto-antonym. The following sentences reflect the distinction in meaning:

- In response to North Korea's latest nuclear weapons test, world leaders have called for harsher sanctions to punish the country for its actions.

- The general has sanctioned a withdrawal of troops from the area.

A context clue can be found in sentence A, which mentions "to punish." A punishment is similar to a penalty, so sentence A is using the word *sanction* according to this definition.

Other examples of auto-antonyms include *oversight*—"to supervise something" or "a missed detail"), *resign*—"to quit" or "to sign again, as a contract," and *screen*—"to show" or "to conceal." For these types of words, recognizing context clues is an important way to avoid misinterpreting the sentence's meaning.

Syntax

Syntax refers to the arrangement of words, phrases, and clauses to form a sentence. Knowledge of syntax can also give insight into a word's meaning. The section above considered several examples using the word *reservation* and applied context clues to determine the word's appropriate meaning in each sentence. Here is an example of how the placement of a word can impact its meaning and grammatical function:

- The development team has reserved the conference room for today.

- Her quiet and reserved nature is sometimes misinterpreted as unfriendliness when people first meet her.

In addition to using *reserved* to mean different things, each sentence also uses the word to serve a different grammatical function. In sentence A, *reserved* is part of the verb phrase *has reserved*, indicating the meaning "to set aside for a particular use." In sentence B, *reserved* acts as a modifier within the noun phrase "her quiet and reserved nature." Because the word is being used as an adjective to describe a personality characteristic, it calls up a different definition of the word—"restrained or lacking familiarity with others." As this example shows, the function of a word within the overall sentence structure can allude to its meaning. It is also useful to refer to the earlier chart about suffixes and parts of speech as another clue into what grammatical function a word is serving in a sentence.

Analyzing Nuances of Word Meaning and Figures of Speech

By now, it should be apparent that language is not as simple as one word directly correlated to one meaning. Rather, one word can express a vast array of diverse meanings, and similar meanings can be expressed through different words. However, there are very few words that express exactly the same meaning. For this reason, it is important to be able to pick up on the nuances of word meaning.

Many words contain two levels of meaning: connotation and denotation as discussed previously in the informational texts and rhetoric section. A word's *denotation* is its most literal meaning—the definition that can readily be found in the dictionary. A word's *connotation* includes all of its emotional and cultural associations.

In literary writing, authors rely heavily on connotative meaning to create mood and characterization. The following are two descriptions of a rainstorm:

- The rain slammed against the windowpane and the wind howled through the fireplace. A pair of hulking oaks next to the house cast eerie shadows as their branches trembled in the wind.

- The rain pattered against the windowpane and the wind whistled through the fireplace. A pair of stately oaks next to the house cast curious shadows as their branches swayed in the wind.

Description A paints a creepy picture for readers with strongly emotional words like *slammed*, connoting force and violence. *Howled* connotes pain or wildness, and *eerie* and *trembled* connote fear. Overall, the connotative language in this description serves to inspire fear and anxiety.

However, as can be seen in description B, swapping out a few key words for those with different connotations completely changes the feeling of the passage. *Slammed* is replaced with the more cheerful *pattered*, and *hulking* has been swapped out for *stately*. Both words imply something large, but *hulking* is more intimidating whereas *stately* is more respectable. *Curious* and *swayed* seem more playful than the language used in the earlier description. Although both descriptions represent roughly the same situation, the nuances of the emotional language used throughout the passages create a very different sense for readers.

Selective choice of connotative language can also be extremely impactful in other forms of writing, such as editorials or persuasive texts. Through connotative language, writers reveal their biases and opinions while trying to inspire feelings and actions in readers:

1. Parents won't stop complaining about standardized tests.
2. Parents continue to raise concerns about standardized tests.

Readers should be able to identify the nuance in meaning between these two sentences. The first one carries a more negative feeling, implying that parents are being bothersome or whiny. Readers of the second sentence, though, might come away with the feeling that parents are concerned and involved in their children's education. Again, the aggregate of even subtle cues can combine to give a specific emotional impression to readers, so from an early age, students should be aware of how language can be used to influence readers' opinions.

Another form of non-literal expression can be found in *figures of speech*. As with connotative language, figures of speech tend to be shared within a cultural group and may be difficult to pick up on for learners outside of that group. In some cases, a figure of speech may be based on the literal denotation of the words it contains, but in other cases, a figure of speech is far removed from its literal meaning. A case in point is *irony*, where what is said is the exact opposite of what is meant:

> The new tax plan is poorly planned, based on faulty economic data, and unable to address the financial struggles of middle class families. Yet legislators remain committed to passing this brilliant proposal.

When the writer refers to the proposal as brilliant, the opposite is implied—the plan is "faulty" and "poorly planned." By using irony, the writer means that the proposal is anything but brilliant by using the word in a non-literal sense.

Another figure of speech is *hyperbole*—extreme exaggeration or overstatement. Statements like, "I love you to the moon and back" or "Let's be friends for a million years" utilize hyperbole to convey a greater depth of emotion, without literally committing oneself to space travel or a life of immortality.

Figures of speech may sometimes use one word in place of another. *Synecdoche*, for example, uses a part of something to refer to its whole. The expression "Don't hurt a hair on her head!" implies protecting more than just an individual hair, but rather her entire body. "The art teacher is training a class of Picassos" uses Picasso, one individual notable artist, to stand in for the entire category of talented artists. Another figure of speech using word replacement is *metonymy*, where a word is replaced with something closely associated to it. For example, news reports may use the word "Washington" to refer to the American government or "the crown" to refer to the British monarch.

Meaning of Words in Context

There will be many occasions in one's reading career in which an unknown word or a word with multiple meanings will pop up. There are ways of determining what these words or phrases mean that do not require the use of the dictionary, which is especially helpful during a test where one may not be available. Even outside of the exam, knowing how to derive an understanding of a word via context clues will be a critical skill in the real world. The context is the circumstances in which a story or a passage is happening, and can usually be found in the series of words directly before or directly after the word or phrase in question. The clues are the words that hint towards the meaning of the unknown word or phrase.

There may be questions that ask about the meaning of a particular word or phrase within a passage. There are a couple ways to approach these kinds of questions:

1. Define the word or phrase in a way that is easy to comprehend (using context clues).
2. Try out each answer choice in place of the word.

To demonstrate, here's an example from *Alice in Wonderland*:

Alice was beginning to get very tired of sitting by her sister on the bank, and of having nothing to do: once or twice she <u>peeped</u> into the book her sister was reading, but it had no pictures or conversations in it, "and what is the use of a book," thought Alice, "without pictures or conversations?"

Q: As it is used in the selection, the word <u>peeped</u> means:

Using the first technique, before looking at the answers, define the word "peeped" using context clues and then find the matching answer. Then, analyze the entire passage in order to determine the meaning, not just the surrounding words.

To begin, imagine a blank where the word should be and put a synonym or definition there: "once or twice she _____ into the book her sister was reading." The context clue here is the book. It may be tempting to put "read" where the blank is, but notice the preposition word, "into." One does not read *into* a book, one simply reads a book, and since reading a book requires that it is seen with a pair of eyes, then "look" would make the most sense to put into the blank: "once or twice she <u>looked</u> into the book her sister was reading."

Once an easy-to-understand word or synonym has been supplanted, readers should check to make sure it makes sense with the rest of the passage. What happened after she looked into the book? She thought to herself how a book without pictures or conversations is useless. This situation in its entirety makes sense.

Now check the answer choices for a match:
    a. To make a high-pitched cry
    b. To smack
    c. To look curiously
    d. To pout

Since the word was already defined, Choice C is the best option.

Using the second technique, replace the figurative blank with each of the answer choices and determine which one is the most appropriate. Remember to look further into the passage to clarify that they work, because they could still make sense out of context.

   a. Once or twice she <u>made a high pitched cry</u> into the book her sister was reading
   b. Once or twice she <u>smacked</u> into the book her sister was reading
   c. Once or twice she <u>looked curiously</u> into the book her sister was reading
   d. Once or twice she <u>pouted</u> into the book her sister was reading

For Choice A, it does not make much sense in any context for a person to yell into a book, unless maybe something terrible has happened in the story. Given that afterward Alice thinks to herself how useless a book without pictures is, this option does not make sense within context.

For Choice B, smacking a book someone is reading may make sense if the rest of the passage indicates a reason for doing so. If Alice was angry or her sister had shoved it in her face, then maybe smacking the book would make sense within context. However, since whatever she does with the book causes her to think, "what is the use of a book without pictures or conversations?" then answer Choice B is not an appropriate answer. Answer Choice C fits well within context, given her subsequent thoughts on the matter. Answer Choice D does not make sense in context or grammatically, as people do not "pout into" things.

This is a simple example to illustrate the techniques outlined above. There may, however, be a question in which all of the definitions are correct and also make sense out of context, in which the appropriate context clues will really need to be honed in on in order to determine the correct answer. For example, here is another passage from *Alice in Wonderland*:

> . . . but when the Rabbit actually took a watch out of its waistcoat pocket, and looked at it, and then hurried on, Alice <u>started</u> to her feet, for it flashed across her mind that she had never before seen a rabbit with either a waistcoat-pocket or a watch to take out of it, and burning with curiosity, she ran across the field after it, and was just in time to see it pop down a large rabbit-hole under the hedge.

Q: As it is used in the passage, the word started means
   a. To turn on
   b. To begin
   c. To move quickly
   d. To be surprised

All of these words qualify as a definition of "start," but using context clues, the correct answer can be identified using one of the two techniques above. It's easy to see that one does not turn on, begin, or be surprised to one's feet. The selection also states that she "ran across the field after it," indicating that she was in a hurry. Therefore, to move quickly would make the most sense in this context.

The same strategies can be applied to vocabulary that may be completely unfamiliar. In this case, focus on the words before or after the unknown word in order to determine its definition. Take this sentence, for example:

> Sam was such a <u>miser</u> that he forced Andrew to pay him twelve cents for the candy, even though he had a large inheritance and he knew his friend was poor.

Unlike with assertion questions, for vocabulary questions, it may be necessary to apply some critical thinking skills that may not be explicitly stated within the passage. Think about the implications of the passage, or what the text is trying to say. With this example, it is important to realize that it is considered unusually stingy for a person to demand so little money from someone instead of just letting their friend have the candy, especially if this person is already wealthy. Hence, a <u>miser</u> is a greedy or stingy individual.

Questions about complex vocabulary may not be explicitly asked, but this is a useful skill to know. If there is an unfamiliar word while reading a passage and its definition goes unknown, it is possible to miss out on a critical message that could inhibit the ability to appropriately answer the questions. Practicing this technique in daily life will sharpen this ability to derive meanings from context clues with ease.

Transitional Words and Phrases

There are approximately 200 transitional words and phrases that are commonly used in the English language. Below are lists of common transition words and phrases used throughout transitions.

Time
- after
- before
- during
- in the middle

Example about to be Given
- for example
- in fact
- for instance

Compare
- likewise
- also

Contrast
- however
- yet
- but

Addition
- and
- also
- furthermore
- moreover

Logical Relationships
- if
- then
- therefore
- as a result
- since

Steps in a Process
- first
- second
- last

Transitional words and phrases are important writing devices because they connect sentences and paragraphs. Transitional words and phrases present logical order to writing and provide more coherent meaning to readers.

Transition words can be categorized based on the relationships they create between ideas:

- General order: signaling elaboration of an idea to emphasize a point—e.g., for example, for instance, to demonstrate, including, such as, in other words, that is, in fact, also, furthermore, likewise, and, truly, so, surely, certainly, obviously, doubtless

- Chronological order: referencing the time frame in which main event or idea occurs—e.g., before, after, first, while, soon, shortly thereafter, meanwhile

- *Numerical order/order of importance*: indicating that related ideas, supporting details, or events will be described in a sequence, possibly in order of importance—e.g., *first, second, also, finally, another, in addition, equally important, less importantly, most significantly, the main reason, last but not least*

- *Spatial order*: referring to the space and location of something or where things are located in relation to each other—e.g., *inside, outside, above, below, within, close, under, over, far, next to, adjacent to*

- Cause and effect order: signaling a causal relationship between events or ideas—e.g., thus, therefore, since, resulted in, for this reason, as a result, consequently, hence, for, so

- Compare and contrast order: identifying the similarities and differences between two or more objects, ideas, or lines of thought—e.g., like, as, similarly, equally, just as, unlike, however, but, although, conversely, on the other hand, on the contrary

- Summary order: indicating that a particular idea is coming to a close—e.g., in conclusion, to sum up, in other words, ultimately, above all.

How an Author's Word Choice Shapes Meaning, Style, and Tone

Authors choose their words carefully in order to artfully depict meaning, style, and tone, which is most commonly inferred through the use of adjectives and verbs. The *tone* is the predominant emotion present in the text, and represents the attitude or feelings that an author has towards a character or event.

To review, an adjective is a word used to describe something, and usually precedes the noun, a person, place, or object. A verb is a word describing an action. For example, the sentence "The scary woodpecker ate the spider" includes the adjective "scary," the noun "woodpecker," and the verb "ate." Reading this sentence may rouse some negative feelings, as the word "scary" carries a negative charge. The *charge* is the emotional connotation that can be derived from the adjectives and verbs and is either positive or negative. Recognizing the charge of a particular sentence or passage is an effective way to understand the meaning and tone the author is trying to convey.

Many authors have conflicting charges within the same text, but a definitive tone can be inferred by understanding the meaning of the charges relative to each other. It's important to recognize key conjunctions, or words that link sentences or clauses together. There are several types and subtypes of conjunctions. Three are most important for reading comprehension:

- *Cumulative conjunctions* add one statement to another.
- Examples: and, both, also, as well as, not only
- I.e. The juice is sweet *and* sour.
- *Adversative conjunctions* are used to contrast two clauses.
- Examples: but, while, still, yet, nevertheless
- I.e. She was tired *but* she was happy.
- *Alternative conjunctions* express two alternatives.
- Examples: or, either, neither, nor, else, otherwise
- I.e. He must eat *or* he will die.

Identifying the meaning and tone of a text can be accomplished with the following techniques:

- Identify the adjectives and verbs.
- Recognize any important conjunctions.
- Label the adjectives and verbs as positive or negative.
- Understand what the charge means about the text.

To demonstrate these steps, examine the following passage from the classic children's poem, "The Sheep":

> Lazy sheep, pray tell me why
>
> In the pleasant fields you lie,
>
> Eating grass, and daisies white,
>
> From the morning till the night?
>
> Everything can something do,
>
> But what kind of use are you?
>
> –Taylor, Jane and Ann. "The Sheep."

This selection is a good example of conflicting charges that work together to express an overall tone. Following the first two steps, identify the adjectives, verbs, and conjunctions within the passage. For this example, the adjectives are underlined, the verbs are in **bold**, and the conjunctions *italicized*:

Lazy sheep, pray **tell** me why

In the pleasant fields you **lie**,

Eating grass, and daisies white,

From the morning till the night?

Everything can something do,

But what kind of use are you?

For step three, read the passage and judge whether feelings of positivity or negativity arose. Then assign a charge to each of the words that were outlined. This can be done in a table format, or simply by writing a + or − next to the word.

The word lazy carries a negative connotation; it usually denotes somebody unwilling to work. To **tell** someone something has an exclusively neutral connotation, as it depends on what's being told, which has not yet been revealed at this point, so a charge can be assigned later. The word pleasant is an inherently positive word. To **lie** could be positive or negative depending on the context, but as the subject (the sheep) is lying in a pleasant field, then this is a positive experience. **Eating** is also generally positive.

After labeling the charges for each word, it might be inferred that the tone of this poem is happy and maybe even admiring or innocuously envious. However, notice the adversative conjunction, "but" and what follows. The author has listed all the pleasant things this sheep gets to do all day, but the tone changes when the author asks, "What kind of use are you?" Asking someone to prove their value is a rather hurtful thing to do, as it implies that the person asking the question doesn't believe the subject has any value, so this could be listed under negative charges. Referring back to the verb **tell**, after reading the whole passage, it can be deduced that the author is asking the sheep to tell what use the sheep is, so this has a negative charge.

+	−
• Pleasant • Lie in fields • From morning to night	• Lazy • Tell me • What kind of use are you

Upon examining the charges, it might seem like there's an even amount of positive and negative emotion in this selection, and that's where the conjunction "but" becomes crucial to identifying the tone. The conjunction "but" indicates there's a contrasting view to the pleasantness of the sheep's daily life, and this view is that the sheep is lazy and useless, which is also indicated by the first line, "lazy sheep, pray tell me why."

It might be helpful to look at questions pertaining to tone. For this selection, consider the following question:

The author of the poem regards the sheep with a feeling of what?
    a. Respect
    b. Disgust
    c. Apprehension
    d. Intrigue

Considering the author views the sheep as lazy with nothing to offer, Choice *A* appears to reflect the opposite of what the author is feeling.

Choice *B* seems to mirror the author's feelings towards the sheep, as laziness is considered a disreputable trait, and people (or personified animals, in this case) with unfavorable traits might be viewed with disgust.

Choice *C* doesn't make sense within context, as laziness isn't usually feared.

Choice *D* is tricky, as it may be tempting to argue that the author is intrigued with the sheep because they ask, "pray tell me why." This is another out-of-scope answer choice as it doesn't *quite* describe the feelings the author experiences and there's also a much better fit in Choice *B*.

Inferences in a Text

Readers should be able to make *inferences*. Making an inference requires the reader to read between the lines and look for what is *implied* rather than what is directly stated. That is, using information that is known from the text, the reader is able to make a logical assumption about information that is *not* directly stated but is probably true. Read the following passage:

"Hey, do you wanna meet my new puppy?" Jonathan asked.

"Oh, I'm sorry but please don't—" Jacinta began to protest, but before she could finish, Jonathan had already opened the passenger side door of his car and a perfect white ball of fur came bouncing towards Jacinta.

"Isn't he the cutest?" beamed Jonathan.

"Yes—achoo!—he's pretty—aaaachooo!!—adora—aaa—aaaachoo!" Jacinta managed to say in between sneezes. "But if you don't mind, I—I—achoo!—need to go inside."

Which of the following can be inferred from Jacinta's reaction to the puppy?
    a. she hates animals
    b. she is allergic to dogs
    c. she prefers cats to dogs
    d. she is angry at Jonathan

An inference requires the reader to consider the information presented and then form their own idea about what is probably true. Based on the details in the passage, what is the best answer to the question? Important details to pay attention to include the tone of Jacinta's dialogue, which is overall polite and apologetic, as well as her reaction itself, which is a long string of sneezes. Answer choices (a) and (d) both express strong emotions ("hates" and "angry") that are not evident in Jacinta's speech or actions. Answer choice (c) mentions cats, but there is nothing in the passage to indicate Jacinta's feelings about cats. Answer choice (b), "she is allergic to dogs," is the most logical choice—based on the fact that she began sneezing as soon as a fluffy dog approached her, it makes sense to guess that Jacinta might be allergic to dogs. So even though Jacinta never directly states, "Sorry, I'm allergic to dogs!" using the clues in the passage, it is still reasonable to guess that this is true.

Making inferences is crucial for readers of literature, because literary texts often avoid presenting complete and direct information to readers about characters' thoughts or feelings, or they present this information in an unclear way, leaving it up to the reader to interpret clues given in the text. In order to make inferences while reading, readers should ask themselves:

- What details are being presented in the text?
- Is there any important information that seems to be missing?
- Based on the information that the author *does* include, what else is probably true?
- Is this inference reasonable based on what is already known?

Drawing Conclusions

Determining conclusions requires being an active reader, as a reader must make a prediction and analyze facts to identify a conclusion. There are a few ways to determine a logical conclusion, but careful reading is the most important. It's helpful to read a passage a few times, noting details that seem important to the piece. A reader should also identify key words in a passage to determine the logical conclusion or determination that flows from the information presented.

Textual evidence within the details helps readers draw a conclusion about a passage. *Textual evidence* refers to information—facts and examples that support the main point. Textual evidence will likely come from outside sources and can be in the form of quoted or paraphrased material. In order to draw a conclusion from evidence, it's important to examine the credibility and validity of that evidence as well as how (and if) it relates to the main idea.

If an author presents a differing opinion or a *counter-argument* in order to refute it, the reader should consider how and why this information is being presented. It is meant to strengthen the original argument and shouldn't be confused with the author's intended conclusion, but it should also be considered in the reader's final evaluation.

Sometimes, authors explicitly state the conclusion they want readers to understand. Alternatively, a conclusion may not be directly stated. In that case, readers must rely on the implications to form a logical conclusion:

> On the way to the bus stop, Michael realized his homework wasn't in his backpack. He ran back to the house to get it and made it back to the bus just in time.

In this example, though it's never explicitly stated, it can be inferred that Michael is a student on his way to school in the morning. When forming a conclusion from implied information, it's important to read the text carefully to find several pieces of evidence in the text to support the conclusion.

Summarizing is an effective way to draw a conclusion from a passage. A summary is a shortened version of the original text, written by the reader in his/her own words. Focusing on the main points of the original text and including only the relevant details can help readers reach a conclusion. It's important to retain the original meaning of the passage.

Like summarizing, *paraphrasing* can also help a reader fully understand different parts of a text. Paraphrasing calls for the reader to take a small part of the passage and list or describe its main points. Paraphrasing is more than rewording the original passage, though. It should be written in the reader's own words, while still retaining the meaning of the original source. This will indicate an understanding of the original source, yet still help the reader expand on his/her interpretation.

Readers should pay attention to the *sequence*, or the order in which details are laid out in the text, as this can be important to understanding its meaning as a whole. Writers will often use transitional words to help the reader understand the order of events and to stay on track. Words like *next, then, after*, and *finally* show that the order of events is important to the author. In some cases, the author omits these transitional words, and the sequence is implied. Authors may even purposely present the information out of order to make an impact or have an effect on the reader. An example might be when a narrative writer uses *flashback* to reveal information.

There are several ways readers can draw conclusions from authors' ideas, such as note taking, text evidence, text credibility, writing a response to text, directly stated information versus implications, outlining, summarizing, and paraphrasing. Let's take a look at each important strategy to help readers draw logical conclusions.

Note Taking
When readers take notes throughout texts or passages, they are jotting down important facts or points that the author makes. Note taking is a useful record of information that helps readers understand the text or passage and respond to it. When taking notes, readers should keep lines brief and filled with pertinent information so that they are not rereading a large amount of text, but rather just key points, elements, or words. After readers have completed a text or passage, they can refer to their notes to help them form a conclusion about the author's ideas in the text or passage.

Text Evidence
Text evidence is the information readers find in a text or passage that supports the main idea or point(s) in a story. In turn, text evidence can help readers draw conclusions about the text or passage. The information should be taken directly from the text or passage and placed in quotation marks. Text evidence provides readers with information to support ideas about the text so that they do not rely simply on their own thoughts. Details should be precise, descriptive, and factual. Statistics are a great piece of text evidence because they provide readers with exact numbers and not just a generalization. For example, instead of saying "Asia has a larger population than Europe," authors could provide detailed information such as, "In Asia there are over 4 billion people, whereas in Europe there are a little over 750 million." More definitive information provides better evidence to readers to help support their conclusions about texts or passages.

Text Credibility
Credible sources are important when drawing conclusions because readers need to be able to trust what they are reading. Authors should always use credible sources to help gain the trust of their readers. A text is *credible* when it is believable and the author is objective and unbiased. If readers do not trust an author's words, they may simply dismiss the text completely. For example, if an author writes a persuasive essay, he or she is outwardly trying to sway readers' opinions to align with his or her own. Readers may agree or disagree with the author, which may, in turn, lead them to believe that the author is credible or not credible. Also, readers should keep in mind the source of the text. If readers review a journal about astronomy, would a more reliable source be a NASA employee or a medical doctor?

Overall, text credibility is important when drawing conclusions, because readers want reliable sources that support the decisions they have made about the author's ideas.

Writing a Response to Text

Once readers have determined their opinions and validated the credibility of a text, they can then reflect on the text. Writing a response to a text is one way readers can reflect on the given text or passage. When readers write responses to a text, it is important for them to rely on the evidence within the text to support their opinions or thoughts. Supporting evidence such as facts, details, statistics, and quotes directly from the text are key pieces of information readers should reflect upon or use when writing a response to text.

Directly Stated Information Versus Implications

Engaged readers should constantly self-question while reviewing texts to help them form conclusions. Self-questioning is when readers review a paragraph, page, passage, or chapter and ask themselves, "Did I understand what I read?," "What was the main event in this section?," "Where is this taking place?," and so on. Authors can provide clues or pieces of evidence throughout a text or passage to guide readers toward a conclusion. This is why active and engaged readers should read the text or passage in its entirety before forming a definitive conclusion. If readers do not gather all the pieces of evidence needed, then they may jump to an illogical conclusion.

At times, authors directly state conclusions while others simply imply them. Of course, it is easier if authors outwardly provide conclusions to readers, because it does not leave any information open to interpretation. On the other hand, implications are things that authors do not directly state but can be assumed based off of information they provided. If authors only imply what may have happened, readers can form a menagerie of ideas for conclusions. For example, look at the following statement: "Once we heard the sirens, we hunkered down in the storm shelter." In this statement, the author does not directly state that there was a tornado, but clues such as "sirens" and "storm shelter" provide insight to the readers to help form that conclusion.

Outlining

An outline is a system used to organize writing. When reading texts, outlining is important because it helps readers organize important information in a logical pattern using roman numerals. Usually, outlines start with the main idea(s) and then branch out into subgroups or subsidiary thoughts of subjects. Not only do outlines provide a visual tool for readers to reflect on how events, characters, settings, or other key parts of the text or passage relate to one another, but they can also lead readers to a stronger conclusion.

The sample below demonstrates what a general outline looks like.

    I.   Main Topic 1
        a. Subtopic 1
        b. Subtopic 2
            1. Detail 1
            2. Detail 2
   II.   Main Topic 2
        a. Subtopic 1
        b. Subtopic 2
            1. Detail 1
            2. Detail 2

Summarizing

At the end of a text or passage, it is important to summarize what the readers read. Summarizing is a strategy in which readers determine what is important throughout the text or passage, shorten those ideas, and rewrite or retell it in their own words. A summary should identify the main idea of the text or passage. Important details or supportive evidence should also be accurately reported in the summary. If writers provide irrelevant details in the summary, it may cloud the greater meaning of the summary in the text. When summarizing, writers should not include their opinions, quotes, or what they thought the author should have said. A clear summary provides clarity of the text or passage to the readers. Let's review the checklist of items writers should include in their summary.

Summary Checklist
- Title of the story
- Someone: Who is or are the main character(s)?
- Wanted: What did the character(s) want?
- But: What was the problem?
- So: How did the character(s) solve the problem?
- Then: How did the story end? What was the resolution?

Paraphrasing

Another strategy readers can use to help them fully comprehend a text or passage is paraphrasing. Paraphrasing is when readers take the author's words and put them into their own words. When readers and writers paraphrase, they should avoid copying the text—that is plagiarism. It is also important to include as many details as possible when restating the facts. Not only will this help readers and writers recall information, but by putting the information into their own words, they demonstrate whether or not they fully comprehend the text or passage. Look at the example below showing an original text and how to paraphrase it.

Original Text: Fenway Park is home to the beloved Boston Red Sox. The stadium opened on April 20, 1912. The stadium currently seats over 37,000 fans, many of whom travel from all over the country to experience the iconic team and nostalgia of Fenway Park.

Paraphrased: On April 20, 1912, Fenway Park opened. Home to the Boston Red Sox, the stadium now seats over 37,000 fans. Many spectators travel to watch the Red Sox and experience the spirit of Fenway Park.

Paraphrasing, summarizing, and quoting can often cross paths with one another. Review the chart below showing the similarities and differences between the three strategies.

Paraphrasing	Summarizing	Quoting
Uses own words	Puts main ideas into own words	Uses words that are identical to text
References original source	References original source	Requires quotation marks
Uses own sentences	Shows important ideas of source	Uses author's own words and ideas

The Purpose of a Passage

When it comes to an author's writing, readers should always identify a position or stance. No matter how objective a text may seem, readers should assume the author has preconceived beliefs. One can reduce the likelihood of accepting an invalid argument by looking for multiple articles on the topic, including those with varying opinions. If several opinions point in the same direction and are backed by reputable peer-reviewed sources, it's more likely the author has a valid argument. Positions that run contrary to widely held beliefs and existing data should invite scrutiny. There are exceptions to the rule, so be a careful consumer of information.

Though themes, symbols, and motifs are buried deep within the text and can sometimes be difficult to infer, an author's purpose is usually obvious from the beginning. No matter the genre or format, all authors are writing to persuade, inform, entertain, or express feelings. Often, these purposes are blended, with one dominating the rest. It's useful to learn to recognize the author's intent.

Persuasive writing is used to persuade or convince readers of something. It often contains two elements: the argument and the counterargument. The argument takes a stance on an issue, while the counterargument pokes holes in the opposition's stance. Authors rely on logic, emotion, and writer credibility to persuade readers to agree with them. If readers are opposed to the stance before reading, they are unlikely to adopt that stance. However, those who are undecided or committed to the same stance are more likely to agree with the author.

Informative writing tries to teach or inform. Workplace manuals, instructor lessons, statistical reports and cookbooks are examples of informative texts. Informative writing is usually based on facts and is often void of emotion and persuasion. Informative texts generally contain statistics, charts, and graphs. Though most informative texts lack a persuasive agenda, readers must examine the text carefully to determine whether one exists within a given passage.

Stories or narratives are designed to entertain. When you go to the movies, you often want to escape for a few hours, not necessarily to think critically. Entertaining writing is designed to delight and engage the reader. However, sometimes this type of writing can be woven into more serious materials, such as persuasive or informative writing to hook the reader before transitioning into a more scholarly discussion.

Emotional writing works to evoke the reader's feelings, such as anger, euphoria, or sadness. The connection between reader and author is an attempt to cause the reader to share the author's intended emotion or tone. Sometimes in order to make a piece more poignant, the author simply wants readers to feel emotion that the author has felt. Other times, the author attempts to persuade or manipulate the reader into adopting his stance. While it's okay to sympathize with the author, be aware of the individual's underlying intent.

The various writing styles are usually blended, with one purpose dominating the rest. A persuasive text, for example, might begin with a humorous tale to make readers more receptive to the persuasive message, or a recipe in a cookbook designed to inform might be preceded by an entertaining anecdote that makes the recipes more appealing.

Informational Texts

Informational texts are a category of texts within the genre of nonfiction. Their intent is to inform, and while they do convey a point of view and may include literary devices, they do not utilize other literary elements, such as characters or plot. An informational text also reflects a *thesis*—an implicit or explicit statement of the text's intent and/or a *main idea*—the overarching focus and/or purpose of the text, generally implied. Some examples of informational texts are informative articles, instructional/how-to texts, factual reports, reference texts, and self-help texts.

Organizational Structure within Informational Text

When reading informational text, it is important that readers are able to understand its organizational structure as the structure often directly relates to an author's intent to inform and/or persuade the reader. Informational text is specifically designed to relate factual information, and although it is open to a reader's interpretation and application of the facts, the structure of the presentation is carefully designed to lead the reader to a particular conclusion.

The first step in identifying the text's structure is to determine the thesis or main idea. The thesis statement and organization of a work are closely intertwined. *A thesis statement* indicates the writer's purpose and may include the scope and direction of the text. It may be presented at the beginning of a text or at the end, and it may be explicit or implicit.

Once a reader has a grasp of the thesis or main idea of the text, he or she can better determine its organizational structure. Test takers are advised to read informational text passages more than once in order to comprehend the material fully. The following questions should be considered when considering structure:

- How does the author assemble the parts to make an effective whole argument?
- Is the passage linear in nature and if so, what is the timeline or thread of logic?
- What is the presented order of events, facts, or arguments? Are these effective in contributing to the author's thesis?
- How can the passage be divided into sections? How are they related to each other and to the main idea or thesis?
- What key terms are used to indicate the organization?

Next, test takers should skim the passage, noting the first line or two of each body paragraph—the *topic sentences*—and the conclusion. Key *transitional terms*, such as *on the other hand, also, because, however, therefore, most importantly*, and *first*, within the text can also signal organizational structure.

Based on these clues, readers should then be able to identify what type of organizational structure is being used. The following organizational structures are most common:

- *Problem/solution*—organized by an analysis/overview of a problem, followed by potential solution(s)

- *Cause/effect*—organized by the effects resulting from a cause or the cause(s) of a particular effect

- *Spatial order*—organized by points that suggest location or direction—e.g., top to bottom, right to left, outside to inside

- *Chronological/sequence order*—organized by points presented to indicate a passage of time or through purposeful steps/stages

- *Comparison/Contrast*—organized by points that indicate similarities and/or differences between two things or concepts

- *Order of importance*—organized by priority of points, often most significant to least significant or vice versa

Textual Evidence Support in Informational Text

Once a reader has determined an author's thesis or main idea, he or she will need to understand how textual evidence supports interpretation of that thesis or main idea. Test takers will be asked direct questions regarding an author's main idea and may be asked to identify evidence that would support those ideas. This will require test takers to comprehend literal and figurative meanings within the text passage, be able to draw inferences from provided information, and be able to separate important evidence from minor supporting detail. It's often helpful to skim test questions and answer options prior to critically reading informational text; however, test takers should avoid the temptation to solely look for the correct answers. Just trying to find the "right answer" may cause test takers to miss important supporting textual evidence. Making mental note of test questions is only helpful as a guide when reading.

After identifying an author's thesis or main idea, a test taker should look at the supporting details that the author provides to back up his or her assertions, identifying those additional pieces of information that help expand the thesis. From there, test takers should examine that additional information and related details for credibility, the author's use of outside sources, and be able to point to direct evidence that supports the author's claims. It's also imperative that test takers be able to identify what is strong support and what is merely additional information that is nice to know but not necessary. Being able to make this differentiation will help test takers effectively answer questions regarding an author's use of supporting evidence within informational text.

Inference in Informational Text

Inference refers to the reader's ability to understand the unwritten text, i.e., "read between the lines" in terms of an author's intent or message. The strategy asks that a reader not take everything he or she reads at face value but instead, add his or her own interpretation of what the author seems to be trying to convey. A reader's ability to make inferences relies on his or her ability to think clearly and logically about the text. It does not ask that the reader make wild speculation or guess about the material but demands that he or she be able to come to sound conclusion about the material.

An author's use of less literal words and phrases requires readers to make more inference when they read. Since inference involves *deduction*—deriving conclusions from ideas assumed to be true—there's more room for interpretation. Still, critical readers who employ inference, if careful in their thinking, can still arrive at the logical, sound conclusions the author intends.

Word Choice in Informational Text

An author's choice of words—also referred to as *diction*—helps to convey his or her meaning in a particular way. Through diction, an author can convey a particular tone—e.g., a humorous tone, a serious tone—in order to support the thesis in a meaningful way to the reader.

One aspect of understanding an author's word choice is understanding connotation and denotation.

Connotation is when an author chooses words or phrases that invoke ideas or feelings other than their literal meaning. An example of the use of connotation is the word *cheap*, which suggests something is poor in value or negatively describes a person is reluctant to spend money. When something or someone is described this way, the reader is more inclined to have a particular image or feeling about it or him/her. Thus, connotation can be a very effective language tool in creating emotion and swaying opinion.

Denotation refers to words or phrases that mean exactly what they say. It is helpful when a writer wants to present hard facts or vocabulary terms with which readers may be unfamiliar. Some examples of denotation are the words *inexpensive* and *frugal*. *Inexpensive* refers to the cost of something, not its value, and *frugal* indicates that a person is conscientiously watching his or her spending. These terms do not elicit the same emotions that *cheap* does.

Authors sometimes choose to use both, but what they choose and when they use it is what critical readers need to differentiate. One method isn't inherently better than the other; however, one may create a better effect, depending upon an author's intent. If, for example, an author's purpose is to inform, to instruct, and to familiarize readers with a difficult subject, his or her use of connotation may be helpful. However, it may also undermine credibility and confuse readers. An author who wants to create a credible, scholarly effect in his or her text would most likely use denotation, which emphasizes literal, factual meaning and examples.

Lastly, test takers and critical readers alike should be very aware of technical language used within informational text. *Technical language* refers to terminology that is specific to a particular industry and is best understood by those specializing in that industry. This language is fairly easy to differentiate, since it will most likely be unfamiliar to readers. It's critical to be able to define technical language either by the author's written definition, through the use of an included glossary—if offered—or through context clues that help readers clarify word meaning.

Apply Information

A natural extension of being able to make an inference from a given set of information is also being able to apply that information to a new context. This is especially useful in non-fiction or informative writing. Considering the facts and details presented in the text, readers should consider how the same information might be relevant in a different situation. The following is an example of applying an inferential conclusion to a different context:

> Often, individuals behave differently in large groups than they do as individuals. One example of this is the psychological phenomenon known as the bystander effect. According to the

bystander effect, the more people who witness an accident or crime occur, the less likely each individual bystander is to respond or offer assistance to the victim. A classic example of this is the murder of Kitty Genovese in New York City in the 1960s. Although there were over thirty witnesses to her killing by a stabber, none of them intervened to help Kitty or contact the police.

Considering the phenomenon of the bystander effect, what would probably happen if somebody tripped on the stairs in a crowded subway station?
 a. Everybody would stop to help the person who tripped
 b. Bystanders would point and laugh at the person who tripped
 c. Someone would call the police after walking away from the station
 d. Few if any bystanders would offer assistance to the person who tripped

This question asks readers to apply the information they learned from the passage, which is an informative paragraph about the bystander effect. According to the passage, this is a concept in psychology that describes the way people in groups respond to an accident—the more people are present, the less likely any one person is to intervene. While the passage illustrates this effect with the example of a woman's murder, the question asks readers to apply it to a different context—in this case, someone falling down the stairs in front of many subway passengers. Although this specific situation is not discussed in the passage, readers should be able to apply the general concepts described in the paragraph. The definition of the bystander effect includes any instance of an accident or crime in front of a large group of people. The question asks about a situation that falls within the same definition, so the general concept should still hold true: in the midst of a large crowd, few individuals are likely to actually respond to an accident. In this case, answer choice (d) is the best response.

Critical Thinking Skills

It's important to read any piece of writing critically. The goal is to discover the point and purpose of what the author is writing about through analysis. It's also crucial to establish the point or stance the author has taken on the topic of the piece. After determining the author's perspective, readers can then more effectively develop their own viewpoints on the subject of the piece.

It is important to distinguish between *fact and opinion* when reading a piece of writing. A fact is information that can be proven true. If information can be disproved, it is not a fact. For example, water freezes at or below thirty-two degrees Fahrenheit. An argument stating that water freezes at seventy degrees Fahrenheit cannot be supported by data, and is therefore not a fact. Facts tend to be associated with science, mathematics, and statistics. Opinions are information open to debate. Opinions are often tied to subjective concepts like equality, morals, and rights. They can also be controversial. An affirmative argument for a position—such as gun control—can be just as effective as an opposing argument against it.

Authors often use words like *think, feel, believe,* or *in my opinion* when expressing opinion, but these words won't always appear in an opinion piece, especially if it is formally written. An author's opinion may be backed up by facts, which gives it more credibility, but that opinion should not be taken as fact. A critical reader should be suspect of an author's opinion, especially if it is only supported by other opinions.

Fact	Opinion
There are 9 innings in a game of baseball.	Baseball games run too long.
James Garfield was assassinated on July 2, 1881.	James Garfield was a good president.

| McDonalds has stores in 118 countries. | McDonalds has the best hamburgers. |

Critical readers examine the facts used to support an author's argument. They check the facts against other sources to be sure those facts are correct. They also check the validity of the sources used to be sure those sources are credible, academic, and/or peer- reviewed. Consider that when an author uses another person's opinion to support his or her argument, even if it is an expert's opinion, it is still only an opinion and should not be taken as fact. A strong argument uses valid, measurable facts to support ideas. Even then, the reader may disagree with the argument as it may be rooted in his or her personal beliefs.

An authoritative argument may use the facts to sway the reader. In the example of global warming, many experts differ in their opinions of what alternative fuels can be used to aid in offsetting it. Because of this, a writer may choose to only use the information and expert opinion that supports his or her viewpoint.

If the argument is that wind energy is the best solution, the author will use facts that support this idea. That same author may leave out relevant facts on solar energy. The way the author uses facts can influence the reader, so it's important to consider the facts being used, how those facts are being presented, and what information might be left out.

Critical readers should also look for errors in the argument such as logical fallacies and bias. A *logical fallacy* is a flaw in the logic used to make the argument. Logical fallacies include slippery slope, straw man, and begging the question. Authors can also reflect *bias* if they ignore an opposing viewpoint or present their side in an unbalanced way. A strong argument considers the opposition and finds a way to refute it. Critical readers should look for an unfair or one-sided presentation of the argument and be skeptical, as a bias may be present. Even if this bias is unintentional, if it exists in the writing, the reader should be wary of the validity of the argument.

Readers should also look for the use of *stereotypes,* which refer to specific groups. Stereotypes are often negative connotations about a person or place and should always be avoided. When a critical reader finds stereotypes in a piece of writing, they should immediately be critical of the argument and consider the validity of anything the author presents. Stereotypes reveal a flaw in the writer's thinking and may suggest a lack of knowledge or understanding about the subject.

Facts and Opinions

As mentioned previously, authors write with a purpose. They adjust their writing for an intended audience. It is the readers' responsibility to comprehend the writing style or purpose of the author. When readers understand a writer's purpose, they can then form their own thoughts about the text(s) regardless of whether their thoughts are the same as or different from the author's.

Facts Versus Opinions
Readers need to be aware of the writer's purpose to help discern facts and opinions within texts. A *fact* is a piece of information that is true. It can either prove or disprove claims or arguments presented in texts. Facts cannot be changed or altered. For example, the statement: *Abraham Lincoln was assassinated on April 15, 1865,* is a fact. The date and related events cannot be altered.

Authors not only present facts in their writing to support or disprove their claim(s), but they may also express their opinions. Authors may use factsto support their own opinions, especially in a persuasive text; however, that does not make their opinions facts. An *opinion* is a belief or view formed about something that is not necessarily based on the truth. Opinions often express authors' personal feelings about a subject and use words like *believe, think,* or *feel.* For example, the statement: *Abraham Lincoln was the best president who has ever lived*, expresses the writer's opinion. Not all writers or readers agree or disagree with the statement. Therefore, the statement can be altered or adjusted to express opposing or supporting beliefs, such as "Abraham Lincoln was the worst president who has ever lived" or "I also think Abraham Lincoln was a great president."

When authors include facts and opinions in their writing, readers may be less influenced by the text(s). Readers need to be conscious of the distinction between facts and opinions while going through texts. Not only should the intended audience be vigilant in following authors' thoughts versus valid information, readers need to check the source of the facts presented. Facts should have reliable sources derived from credible outlets like almanacs, encyclopedias, medical journals, and so on.

Counterarguments

If an author presents a differing opinion or a counterargument in order to refute it, the reader should consider how and why this information is being presented. It is meant to strengthen the original argument and shouldn't be confused with the author's intended conclusion, but it should also be considered in the reader's final evaluation.

Authors can also use bias if they ignore the opposing viewpoint or present their side in an unbalanced way. A strong argument considers the opposition and finds a way to refute it. Critical readers should look for an unfair or one-sided presentation of the argument and be skeptical, as a bias may be present. Even if this bias is unintentional, if it exists in the writing, the reader should be wary of the validity of the argument. Readers should also look for the use of stereotypes, which refer to specific groups. Stereotypes are often negative connotations about a person or place, and should always be avoided. When a critical reader finds stereotypes in a piece of writing, they should be critical of the argument, and consider the validity of anything the author presents. Stereotypes reveal a flaw in the writer's thinking and may suggest a lack of knowledge or understanding about the subject.

Author's Use of Evidence to Support Claims

Authors utilize a wide range of techniques to tell a story or communicate information. Readers should be familiar with the most common of these techniques. Techniques of writing are also commonly known as rhetorical devices, and they are some of the evidence that authors use to support claims.

In non-fiction writing, authors employ argumentative techniques to present their opinion to readers in the most convincing way. First of all, persuasive writing usually includes at least one type of appeal: an appeal to logic (logos), emotion (pathos), or credibility and trustworthiness (ethos). When a writer appeals to logic, they are asking readers to agree with them based on research, evidence, and an established line of reasoning. An author's argument might also appeal to readers' emotions, perhaps by including personal stories and anecdotes (a short narrative of a specific event). A final type of appeal, appeal to authority, asks the reader to agree with the author's argument on the basis of their expertise or credentials. Consider three different approaches to arguing the same opinion:

Logic (Logos)
Below is an example of an appeal to logic. The author uses evidence to disprove the logic of the school's rule (the rule was supposed to reduce discipline problems; the number of problems has not been reduced; therefore, the rule is not working) and call for its repeal.

Our school should abolish its current ban on cell phone use on campus. This rule was adopted last year as an attempt to reduce class disruptions and help students focus more on their lessons. However, since the rule was enacted, there has been no change in the number of disciplinary problems in class. Therefore, the rule is ineffective and should be done away with.

Emotion (Pathos)

An author's argument might also appeal to readers' emotions, perhaps by including personal stories and anecdotes.

The next example presents an appeal to emotion. By sharing the personal anecdote of one student and speaking about emotional topics like family relationships, the author invokes the reader's empathy in asking them to reconsider the school rule.

Our school should abolish its current ban on cell phone use on campus. If they aren't able to use their phones during the school day, many students feel isolated from their loved ones. For example, last semester, one student's grandmother had a heart attack in the morning. However, because he couldn't use his cell phone, the student didn't know about his grandmother's accident until the end of the day—when she had already passed away and it was too late to say goodbye. By preventing students from contacting their friends and family, our school is placing undue stress and anxiety on students.

Credibility (Ethos)

Finally, an appeal to authority includes a statement from a relevant expert. In this case, the author uses a doctor in the field of education to support the argument. All three examples begin from the same opinion—the school's phone ban needs to change—but rely on different argumentative styles to persuade the reader.

Our school should abolish its current ban on cell phone use on campus. According to Dr. Bartholomew Everett, a leading educational expert, "Research studies show that cell phone usage has no real impact on student attentiveness. Rather, phones provide a valuable technological resource for learning. Schools need to learn how to integrate this new technology into their curriculum." Rather than banning phones altogether, our school should follow the advice of experts and allow students to use phones as part of their learning.

Informational Graphics

A test taker's ability to draw conclusions from an informational graphic is a sub-skill in displaying one's command of reading evidence. Drawing conclusions requires the reader to consider all information provided in the passage, then to use logic to piece it together to form a reasonably correct resolution. In this case, a test taker must look for facts as well as opinionated statements. Both should be considered in order to arrive at a conclusion. These types of questions test one's ability to conduct logical and analytical thinking.

Identifying data-driven evidence in informational graphics is very similar to analyzing factual information. However, it often involves the use of graphics in order to do so. In these types of questions, the test taker will be presented with a graph, or organizational tool, and asked questions regarding the information it contains. On the following page, review the pie chart organizing percentages of primary occupations of public transportation passengers in US cities.

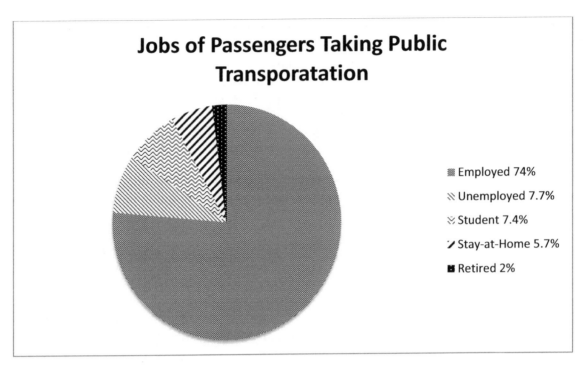

Jobs of Passengers Taking Public Transporatation

- Employed 74%
- Unemployed 7.7%
- Student 7.4%
- Stay-at-Home 5.7%
- Retired 2%

This figure depicts the jobs of passengers taking public transportation in U.S. cities. A corresponding question may have the test taker study the chart, then answer a question regarding the values. For example, is the number of students relying on public transportation greater or less than the number of the unemployed? Similarly, the test may ask if people employed outside the home are less likely to use public transportation than homemakers. Note that the phrase *less likely* may weigh into the reader's choice of optional answers and that the test taker should look for additional passage data to arrive at a conclusion one way or another.

Rhetoric

The IELTS™ Reading section will test a reader's ability to identify an author's use of rhetoric within text passages. Rhetoric is the use of positional or persuasive language to convey one or more central ideas. The idea behind the use of rhetoric is to convince the reader of something. Its use is meant to persuade or motivate the reader. An author may choose to appeal to their audience through logic, emotion, the use of ideology, or by conveying that the central idea is timely, and thus, important to the reader. There are a variety of rhetorical techniques an author can use to achieve this goal.

An author may choose to use traditional elements of style to persuade the reader. They may also use a story's setting, mood, characters, or a central conflict to build emotion in the reader. Similarly, an author may choose to use specific techniques such as alliteration, irony, metaphor, simile, hyperbole, allegory, imagery, onomatopoeia, and personification to persuasively illustrate one or more central ideas they wish the reader to adopt. In order to be successful in a standardized reading comprehension test situation, a reader needs to be well acquainted in recognizing rhetoric and rhetorical devices.

Identifying Elements of Style

A writer's style is unique. The combinations of elements are carefully designed to create an effect on the reader. For example, the novels of J.K. Rowling are very different in style than the novels of Stephen King, yet both are designed to tell a compelling tale and to entertain readers. Furthermore, the articles found in *National Geographic* are vastly different from those a reader may encounter in *People* magazine, yet both have the same objective: to inform the reader. The difference is in the elements of style.

While there are many elements of style an author can employ, it's important to look at three things: the words they choose to use, the voice an author selects, and the fluency of sentence structure. Word choice is critical in persuasive or pictorial writing. While effective authors will choose words that are succinct, different authors will choose various words based on what they are trying to accomplish. For example, a reader would not expect to encounter the same words in a gothic novel that they would read in a scholastic article on gene therapy. An author whose intent is to paint a picture of a foreboding scene, will choose different words than an author who wants to persuade the reader that a particular political party has the most sound, ideological platform. A romance novelist will sound very different than a true crime writer.

The voice an author selects is also important to note. An author's voice is that element of style that indicates their personality. It's important that authors move us as readers; therefore, they will choose a voice that helps them do that. An author's voice may be satirical or authoritative. It may be light-hearted or serious in tone. It may be silly or humorous as well. Voice, as an element of style, can be vague in nature and difficult to identify, since it's also referred to as an author's tone, but it is that element unique to the author. It is the author's "self." A reader can expect an author's voice to vary across literary genres. A non-fiction author will generally employ a more neutral voice than an author of fiction, but use caution when trying to identify voice. Do not confuse an author's voice with a particular character's voice.

Another critical element of style involves how an author structures their sentences. An effective writer—one who wants to paint a vivid picture or strongly illustrate a central idea—will use a variety of sentence structures and sentence lengths. A reader is more likely to be confused if an author uses choppy, unrelated sentences. Similarly, a reader will become bored and lose interest if an author repeatedly uses the same sentence structure. Good writing is fluent. It flows. Varying sentence structure keeps a reader engaged and helps reading comprehension. Consider the following example:

> The morning started off early. It was bright out. It was just daylight. The moon was still in the sky. He was tired from his sleepless night.

Then consider this text:

> Morning hit hard. He didn't remember the last time light hurt this bad. Sleep had been absent, and the very thought of moving towards the new day seemed like a hurdle he couldn't overcome.

Note the variety in sentence structure. The second passage is more interesting to read because the sentence fluency is more effective. Both passages paint the picture of a central character's reaction to dawn, but the second passage is more effective because it uses a variety of sentences and is more fluent than the first.

Elements of style can also include more recognizable components such as a story's setting, the type of narrative an author chooses, the mood they set, and the character conflicts employed. The ability to effectively understand the use of rhetoric demands the reader take note of an author's word choices, writing voice, and the ease of fluency employed to persuade, entertain, illustrate, or otherwise captivate a reader.

<u>Identifying Rhetorical Devices</u>

If one feels strongly about a subject, or has a passion for it, they choose strong words and phrases. Think of the types of rhetoric (or language) our politicians use. Each word, phrase, and idea is carefully crafted to elicit a response. Hopefully, that response is one of agreement to a certain point of view, especially among voters. Authors use the same types of language to achieve the same results. For example, the word "bad" has a certain connotation, but the words "horrid," "repugnant," and "abhorrent" paint a far better picture for the reader. They're more precise. They're interesting to read and they should all illicit stronger feelings in the reader than the word "bad." An author generally uses other devices beyond mere word choice to persuade, convince, entertain, or otherwise engage a reader.

Rhetorical devices are those elements an author utilizes in painting sensory, and hopefully persuasive ideas to which a reader can relate. They are numerable. Test takers will likely encounter one or more standardized test questions addressing varying rhetorical devices. This study guide will address the more common types: alliteration, irony, metaphor, simile, hyperbole, allegory, imagery, onomatopoeia, and personification, providing examples of each.

Alliteration is a device that uses repetitive beginning sounds in words to appeal to the reader. Classic tongue twisters are a great example of alliteration. *She sells sea shells down by the sea shore* is an extreme example of alliteration. Authors will use alliterative devices to capture a reader's attention. It's interesting to note that marketing also utilizes alliteration in the same way. A reader will likely remember products that have the brand name and item starting with the same letter. Similarly, many songs, poems, and catchy phrases use this device. It's memorable. Use of alliteration draws a reader's attention to ideas that an author wants to highlight.

Irony is a device that authors use when pitting two contrasting items or ideas against each other in order to create an effect. It's frequently used when an author wants to employ humor or convey a sarcastic tone. Additionally, it's often used in fictional works to build tension between characters, or between a particular character and the reader. An author may use *verbal irony* (sarcasm), *situational irony* (where actions or events have the opposite effect than what's expected), and *dramatic irony* (where the reader knows something a character does not). Examples of irony include:

- Dramatic Irony: An author describing the presence of a hidden killer in a murder mystery, unbeknownst to the characters but known to the reader.

- Situational Irony: An author relating the tale of a fire captain who loses her home in a five-alarm conflagration.

- Verbal Irony: This is where an author or character says one thing but means another. For example, telling a police officer "Thanks a lot" after receiving a ticket.

Metaphor is a device that uses a figure of speech to paint a visual picture of something that is not literally applicable. Authors relate strong images to readers, and evoke similar strong feelings using metaphors. Most often, authors will mention one thing in comparison to another more familiar to the reader. It's important to note that metaphors do not use the comparative words "like" or "as." At times, metaphors encompass common phrases such as clichés. At other times, authors may use mixed metaphors in making identification between two dissimilar things. Examples of metaphors include:

- An author describing a character's anger as *a flaming sheet of fire.*
- An author relating a politician as having been a folding chair under close questioning.
- A novel's character telling another character to *take a flying hike.*
- Shakespeare's assertion that *all the world's a stage.*

Simile is a device that compares two dissimilar things using the words "like" and "as." When using similes, an author tries to catch a reader's attention and use comparison of unlike items to make a point. Similes are commonly used and often develop into figures of speech and catch phrases. Examples of similes include:

- An author describing a character as having a complexion like a faded lily.

- An investigative journalist describing his interview subject as being like cold steel and with a demeanor hard as ice.

- An author asserting the current political arena is just like a three-ring circus and as dry as day old bread.

Similes and metaphors can be confusing. When utilizing simile, an author will state one thing is like another. A metaphor states one thing is another. An example of the difference would be if an author states a character is *just like a fierce tiger and twice as angry,* as opposed to stating the character *is a fierce tiger and twice as angry.*

Hyperbole is simply an exaggeration that is not taken literally. A potential test taker will have heard or employed hyperbole in daily speech, as it is a common device we all use. Authors will use hyperbole to draw a reader's eye toward important points and to illicit strong emotional and relatable responses. Examples of hyperbole include:

- An author describing a character as being as big as a house and twice the circumference of a city block.

- An author stating the city's water problem as being old as the hills and more expensive than a king's ransom in spent tax dollars.

- A journalist stating the mayoral candidate died of embarrassment when her tax records were made public.

Allegories are stories or poems with hidden meanings, usually a political or moral one. Authors will frequently use allegory when leading the reader to a conclusion. Allegories are similar to parables, symbols, and analogies. Often, an author will employ the use of allegory to make political, historical, moral, or social observations. As an example, Jonathan Swift's work *Gulliver's Travels into Several Remote Nations of the World* is an allegory in and of itself. The work is a political allegory of England during Jonathan Swift's lifetime. Set in the travel journal style plot of a giant amongst smaller people, and a smaller Gulliver amongst the larger, it is a commentary on Swift's political stance of existing issues of his age. Many fictional works are entire allegories in and of themselves. George Orwell's *Animal Farm* is a story of animals that conquer man and form their own farm society with swine at the top; however, it is not a literal story in any sense. It's Orwell's political allegory of Russian society during and after the Communist revolution of 1917. Other examples of allegory in popular culture include:

- Aesop's fable "The Tortoise and the Hare," which teaches readers that being steady is more important than being fast and impulsive.

- The popular *Hunger Games* by Suzanne Collins that teaches readers that media can numb society to what is truly real and important.

- Dr. Seuss's *Yertle the Turtle* which is a warning against totalitarianism and, at the time it was written, against the despotic rule of Adolf Hitler.

Imagery is a rhetorical device that an author employs when they use visual, or descriptive, language to evoke a reader's emotion. Use of imagery as a rhetorical device is broader in scope than this study guide addresses, but in general, the function of imagery is to create a vibrant scene in the reader's imagination and, in turn, tease the reader's ability to identify through strong emotion and sensory experience. In the simplest of terms, imagery, as a rhetoric device, beautifies literature. An example of poetic imagery is below:

> Pain has an element of blank
>
> It cannot recollect
>
> When it began, or if there were
>
> A day when it was not.
>
> It has no future but itself,
>
> Its infinite realms contain
>
> Its past, enlightened to perceive
>
> New periods of pain.

In the above poem, Emily Dickenson uses strong imagery. Pain is equivalent to an "element of blank" or of nothingness. Pain cannot recollect a beginning or end, as if it was a person (see *personification* below). Dickenson appeals to the reader's sense of a painful experience by discussing the unlikelihood that discomfort sees a future, but does visualize a past and present. She simply indicates that pain, through the use of imagery, is cyclical and never ending. Dickenson's theme is one of painful depression and it is through the use of imagery that she conveys this to her readers.

Onomatopoeia is the author's use of words that create sound. Words like *pop* and *sizzle* are examples of onomatopoeia. When an author wants to draw a reader's attention in an auditory sense, they will use onomatopoeia. An author may also use onomatopoeia to create sounds as interjection or commentary.

Examples include:

- An author describing a cat's vocalization as the kitten's chirrup echoed throughout the empty cabin.
- A description of a campfire as crackling and whining against its burning green wood.
- An author relating the sound of a car accident as *metallic screeching against crunching asphalt*.
- A description of an animal roadblock as being *a symphonic melody of groans, baas, and moans*.

Personification is a rhetorical device that an author uses to attribute human qualities to inanimate objects or animals. Once again, this device is useful when an author wants the reader to strongly relate to an idea. As in the example of George Orwell's *Animal Farm*, many of the animals are given the human abilities to speak, reason, apply logic, and otherwise interact as humans do. This helps the reader see how easily it is for any society to segregate into the haves and the have-nots through the manipulation of power. Personification is a device that enables the reader to empathize through human experience.

Examples of personification include:

- An author describing the wind as *whispering through the trees*.

- A description of a stone wall as being a hardened, unmovable creature made of cement and brick.

- An author attributing a city building as having slit eyes and an unapproachable, foreboding façade.

- An author describing spring as a beautiful bride, blooming in white, ready for summer's matrimony.

When identifying rhetorical devices, look for words and phrases that capture one's attention. Make note of the author's use of comparison between the inanimate and the animate. Consider words that make the reader feel sounds and envision imagery. Pay attention to the rhythm of fluid sentences and to the use of words that evoke emotion. The ability to identify rhetorical devices is another step in achieving successful reading comprehension and in being able to correctly answer standardized questions related to those devices.

Analysis of History/Social Studies Excerpts

The IELTS™ Reading section may include historically-based excerpts. The test may also include one or more passages from social sciences such as economics, psychology, or sociology.

For these types of questions, the test taker will need to utilize all the reading comprehension skills discussed above, but mastery of further skills will help. This section addresses those skills.

Comprehending Test Questions Prior to Reading

While preparing for a historical passage on a standardized test, first read the test questions, and then quickly scan the test answers prior to reading the passage itself. Notice there is a difference between the terms *read* and *scans*. Reading involves full concentration while addressing every word. Scanning involves quickly glancing at text in chunks, noting important dates, words, and ideas along the way. Reading test questions will help the test taker know what information to focus on in the historical passage. Scanning answers will help the test taker focus on possible answer options while reading the passage.

When reading standardized test questions that address historical passages, be sure to clearly understand what each question is asking. Is a question asking about vocabulary? Is another asking for the test taker to find a specific historical fact? Do any of the questions require the test taker to draw conclusions, identify an author's topic, tone, or position? Knowing what content to address will help the test taker focus on the information they will be asked about later. However, the test taker should approach this reading comprehension technique with some caution. It is tempting to only look for the right answers within any given passage. Do not put on "reading blinders" and ignore all other information presented in a passage. It is important to fully read every passage and not just scan it. Strictly looking for what may be the right answers to test questions can cause the test taker to ignore important contextual clues that actually require critical thinking in order to identify correct answers. Scanning a passage for what appears to be wrong answers can have a similar result.

When reading test questions prior to tackling a historical passage, be sure to understand what skills the test is assessing, and then fully read the related passage with those skills in mind. Focus on every word in both the test questions and the passage itself. Read with a critical eye and a logical mind.

Reading for Factual Information

Standardized test questions that ask for factual information are usually straightforward. These types of questions will either ask the test taker to confirm a fact by choosing a correct answer, or to select a correct answer based on a negative fact question.

For example, the test taker may encounter a passage from Lincoln's Gettysburg address. A corresponding test question may ask the following:

> Which war is Abraham Lincoln referring to in the following passage?: "Now we are engaged in a great civil war, testing whether that nation, or any nation so conceived and so dedicated, can long endure."

This type of question is asking the test taker to confirm a simple fact. Given options such as World War I, the War of Spanish Succession, World War II, and the American Civil War, the test taker should be able to correctly identify the American Civil War based on the words "civil war" within the passage itself, and, hopefully, through general knowledge. In this case, reading the test question and scanning answer options ahead of reading the Gettysburg address would help quickly identify the correct answer. Similarly, a test taker may be asked to confirm a historical fact based on a negative fact question. For example, a passage's corresponding test question may ask the following:

> Which option is incorrect based on the above passage?

Given a variety of choices speaking about which war Abraham Lincoln was addressing, the test taker would need to eliminate all correct answers pertaining to the American Civil War and choose the answer choice referencing a different war. In other words, the correct answer is the one that contradicts the information in the passage.

It is important to remember that reading for factual information is straightforward. The test taker must distinguish fact from bias. Factual statements can be proven or disproven independent of the author and from a variety of other sources. Remember, successfully answering questions regarding factual information may require the test taker to re-read the passage, as these types of questions test for attention to detail.

Reading for Tone, Message, and Effect

The Reading section does not just address a test taker's ability to find facts within a reading passage; it also determines a reader's ability to determine an author's viewpoint through the use of tone, message, and overall effect. This type of reading comprehension requires inference skills, deductive reasoning skills, the ability to draw logical conclusions, and overall critical thinking skills. Reading for factual information is straightforward. Reading for an author's tone, message, and overall effect is not. It's key to read carefully when asked test questions that address a test taker's ability to these writing devices. These are not questions that can be easily answered by quickly scanning for the right information.

Tone

An author's *tone* is the use of particular words, phrases, and writing style to convey an overall meaning. Tone expresses the author's attitude towards a particular topic. For example, a historical reading passage may begin like the following:

> The presidential election of 1960 ushered in a new era, a new Camelot, a new phase of forward thinking in U.S. politics that embraced brash action, unrest, and responded with admirable leadership.

From this opening statement, a reader can draw some conclusions about the author's attitude towards President John F. Kennedy. Furthermore, the reader can make additional, educated guesses about the state of the Union during the 1960 presidential election. By close reading, the test taker can determine that the repeated use of the word *new* and words such as *admirable leadership* indicate the author's tone of admiration regarding the President's boldness. In addition, the author assesses that the era during President Kennedy's administration was problematic through the use of the words *brash action* and *unrest*. Therefore, if a test taker encountered a test question asking about the author's use of tone and their assessment of the Kennedy administration, the test taker should be able to identify an answer indicating admiration. Similarly, if asked about the state of the Union during the 1960s, a test taker should be able to correctly identify an answer indicating political unrest.

When identifying an author's tone, the following list of words may be helpful. This is not an inclusive list. Generally, parts of speech that indicate attitude will also indicate tone:

- Comical
- Angry
- Ambivalent
- Scary
- Lyrical
- Matter-of-fact
- Judgmental
- Sarcastic
- Malicious
- Objective
- Pessimistic
- Patronizing
- Gloomy
- Instructional
- Satirical
- Formal
- Casual

Message

An author's *message* is the same as the overall meaning of a passage. It is the main idea, or the main concept the author wishes to convey. An author's message may be stated outright or it may be implied. Regardless, the test taker will need to use careful reading skills to identify an author's message or purpose.

Often, the message of a particular passage can be determined by thinking about why the author wrote the information. Many historical passages are written to inform and to teach readers established, factual information. However, many historical works are also written to convey biased ideas to readers. Gleaning bias from an author's message in a historical passage can be difficult, especially if the reader is presented with a variety of established facts as well. Readers tend to accept historical writing as factual. This is not always the case. Any discerning reader who has tackled historical information on topics such as United States political party agendas can attest that two or more works on the same topic may have completely different messages supporting or refuting the value of the identical policies. Therefore, it is important to critically assess an author's message separate from factual information. One author, for example, may point to the rise of unorthodox political candidates in an election year based on the failures of the political party in office while another may point to the rise of the same candidates in the same election year based on the current party's successes. The historical facts of what has occurred leading up to an election year are not in refute. Labeling those facts as a failure or a success is a bias within an author's overall *message*, as is excluding factual information in order to further a particular point. In a standardized testing situation, a reader must be able to critically assess what the author is trying to say separate from the historical facts that surround their message.

Using the example of Lincoln's Gettysburg Address, a test question may ask the following:

What is the message the author is trying to convey through this address?

Then they will ask the test taker to select an answer that best expresses Lincoln's *message* to his audience. Based on the options given, a test taker should be able to select the answer expressing the idea that Lincoln's audience should recognize the efforts of those who died in the war as a sacrifice to preserving human equality and self-government.

Effect

The *effect* an author wants to convey is when an author wants to impart a particular mood in their message. An author may want to challenge a reader's intellect, inspire imagination, or spur emotion. An author may present information to appeal to a physical, aesthetic, or transformational sense. Take the following text as an example:

In 1963, Martin Luther King stated "I have a dream." The gathering at the Lincoln Memorial was the beginning of the Civil Rights movement and, with its reference to the Emancipation Proclamation, electrified those who wanted freedom and equality while rising from hatred and slavery. It was the beginning of radical change.

The test taker may be asked about the effect this statement might have on King's audience. Through careful reading of the passage, the test taker should be able to choose an answer that best identifies an effect of grabbing the audience's attention. The historical facts are in place: King made the speech in 1963 at the Lincoln Memorial, kicked off the civil rights movement, and referenced the Emancipation Proclamation. The words *electrified* and *radical change* indicate the effect the author wants the reader to understand as a result of King's speech. In this historical passage, facts are facts. However, the author's message goes above the facts to indicate the effect the message had on the audience and, in addition, the effect the event should have on the reader.

When reading historical passages, the test taker should perform due diligence in their awareness of the test questions and answers up front. From there, the test taker should carefully, and critically, read all historical excerpts with an eye for detail, tone, message (biased or unbiased), and effect. Being able to synthesize these skills will result in success in a standardized testing situation.

Analysis of Science Excerpts

The Reading section may include passages that address the fundamental concepts of Earth science, biology, chemistry, or other sciences. Again, prior knowledge of these subjects is not necessary to determine correct test answers; instead, the test taker's ability to comprehend the passages is key to success. When reading scientific excerpts, the test taker must be able to examine quantitative information, identify hypotheses, interpret data, and consider implications of the material they are presented with. It is helpful, at this point, to reference the above section on comprehending test questions prior to reading. The same rules apply: read questions and scan questions, along with their answers, prior to fully reading a passage. Be informed prior to approaching a scientific text. A test taker should know what they will be asked and how to apply their reading skills. In this section of the test, it is also likely that a test taker will encounter graphs and charts to assess their ability to interpret scientific data with an appropriate conclusion. This section will determine the skills necessary to address scientific data presented through identifying hypotheses, through reading and examining data, and through interpreting data representation passages.

Examine Hypotheses

When presented with fundamental, scientific concepts, it is important to read for understanding. The most basic skill in achieving this literacy is to understand the concept of hypothesis and moreover, to be able to identify it in a particular passage. A hypothesis is a proposed idea that needs further investigation in order to be proven true or false. While it can be considered an educated guess, a hypothesis goes more in depth in its attempt to explain something that is not currently accepted within scientific theory. It requires further experimentation and data gathering to test its validity and is subject to change, based on scientifically conducted test results. Being able to read a science passage and understand its main purpose, including any hypotheses, helps the test taker understand data-driven evidence. It helps the test taker to be able to correctly answer questions about the science excerpt they are asked to read.

When reading to identify a hypothesis, a test taker should ask, "What is the passage trying to establish? What is the passage's main idea? What evidence does the passage contain that either supports or refutes this idea?" Asking oneself these questions will help identify a hypothesis. Additionally, hypotheses are logical statements that are testable, and use very precise language.

Review the following hypothesis example:

> Consuming excess sugar in the form of beverages has a greater impact on childhood obesity and subsequent weight gain than excessive sugar from food.

While this is likely a true statement, it is still only a conceptual idea in a text passage regarding sugar consumption in childhood obesity, unless the passage also contains tested data that either proves or disproves the statement. A test taker could expect the rest of the passage to cite data proving that children who drink empty calories and don't exercise will, in fact, be obese.

A hypothesis goes further in that, given its ability to be proven or disproven, it may result in further hypotheses that require extended research. For example, the hypothesis regarding sugar consumption in drinks, after undergoing rigorous testing, may lead scientists to state another hypothesis such as the following:

> Consuming excess sugar in the form of beverages as opposed to food items is a habit found in mostly sedentary children.

This new, working hypothesis further focuses not just on the source of an excess of calories, but tries an "educated guess" that empty caloric intake has a direct, subsequent impact on physical behavior.

When reading a science passage to determine its hypothesis, a test taker should look for a concept that attempts to explain a phenomenon, is testable, logical, precisely worded, and yields data-driven results. The test taker should scan the presented passage for any word or data-driven clues that will help identify the hypothesis, and then be able to correctly answer test questions regarding the hypothesis based on their critical thinking skills.

Academic Test Reading Practice Questions

The following passage about the circulatory system would be found in an introductory anatomy and physiology textbook. Read the passage and then answer the associated questions.

(A) The circulatory system is a network of organs and tubes that transport blood, hormones, nutrients, oxygen, and other gases to cells and tissues throughout the body. It is also known as the cardiovascular system. The major components of the circulatory system are the blood vessels, blood, and heart.

(B) In the circulatory system, blood vessels are responsible for transporting blood throughout the body. The blood vessels, in order of decreasing size away from the heart, are arteries, arterioles, and capillaries. Towards the heart, from smallest to largest, are capillaries, venules, and veins.

Arteries carry blood from the heart to the rest of the body. Veins carry blood from the body to the heart. Capillaries connect arteries to veins and form networks that exchange materials between the blood and the cells.

In general, arteries are stronger and thicker than veins, as they withstand high pressures exerted by the blood as the heart pumps it through the body. Arteries control blood flow through either vasoconstriction (narrowing of the blood vessel's diameter) or vasodilation (widening of the blood vessel's diameter). The blood in veins is under much lower pressures, so veins have valves to prevent the backflow of blood.

Most of the exchange between the blood and tissues takes place through the capillaries. There are three types of capillaries: continuous, fenestrated, and sinusoidal.

Continuous capillaries are made up of epithelial cells tightly connected together. As a result, they limit the types of materials that pass into and out of the blood. Continuous capillaries are the most common type of capillary. Fenestrated capillaries have openings that allow materials to be freely exchanged between the blood and tissues. They are commonly found in the digestive, endocrine, and urinary systems. Sinusoidal capillaries have larger openings and allow proteins and blood cells through. They are found primarily in the liver, bone marrow, and spleen.

(C) Blood is vital to the human body. It is a liquid connective tissue that serves as a transport system for supplying cells with nutrients and carrying away their wastes. The average adult human has five to six quarts of blood circulating through their body. Approximately 55% of blood is plasma (the fluid portion), and the remaining 45% is composed of solid cells and cell parts. There are three major types of blood cells: red blood cells, white blood cells, and platelets. Red blood cells transport oxygen throughout the body. They contain a protein called hemoglobin that allows them to carry oxygen. The iron in the hemoglobin gives the cells and the blood their red colors. White blood cells are responsible for fighting infectious diseases and maintaining the immune system. There are five types of white blood cells: neutrophils, lymphocytes, eosinophils, monocytes, and basophils. Platelets are cell fragments which play a central role in the blood clotting process.

All blood cells in adults are produced in the bone marrow—red blood cells from red marrow and white blood cells from yellow marrow.

(D) The heart is a two-part, muscular pump that forcefully pushes blood throughout the human body. The human heart, also called the myocardium, has four chambers—two upper atria and two lower ventricles, a pair on the left and a pair on the right. Anatomically, *left* and *right* correspond to the sides of the body that the patient themselves would refer to as left and right.

Four valves help to section off the chambers from one another. Between the right atrium and ventricle, the three flaps of the tricuspid valve keep blood from backflowing from the ventricle to the atrium, similar to how the two flaps of the mitral valve work between the left atrium and ventricle. As these two valves lie between an atrium and a ventricle, they are referred to as atrioventricular (AV) valves. The other two valves are semilunar (SL) and control blood flow into the two great arteries leaving the ventricles. The pulmonary valve connects the right ventricle to the pulmonary artery while the aortic valve connects the left ventricle to the aorta.

Blood enters the (1) right atrium. When it contracts, blood passes through the (2) tricuspid valve into the (3) right ventricle. After filling, the right ventricle contracts, and the tricuspid valve closes, pushing blood through the (4) pulmonary semilunar valve into the (5) pulmonary arteries. These arteries, unlike all other arteries in the body, carry deoxygenated blood to the lungs, where blood travels through the (6) alveolar capillaries. Here, oxygen is absorbed and carbon dioxide is removed.

The newly-oxygenated blood is carried by the (7) pulmonary veins back to the (8) left atrium. Contraction of the left atrium moves blood through the (9) bicuspid valve into the (10) left ventricle (the largest heart chamber). When the bicuspid valve closes and the left ventricle contracts, blood is forced into the (11) aortic valve through the aorta and on to systemic circulation.

(E) One complete sequence of cardiac activity is referred to as a cardiac cycle. The cardiac cycle represents the relaxation and contraction of the heart and can be divided into two phases: diastole and systole.

Diastole is the phase during which the heart relaxes and fills with blood. It gives rise to the diastolic blood pressure (DBP), which is the bottom number of a blood pressure reading. Systole is the phase during which the heart contracts and discharges blood. It gives rise to the systolic blood pressure (SBP), which is the top number of a blood pressure reading. The heart's electrical conduction system coordinates the cardiac cycle.

(F) The mechanical contraction of the heart is controlled by an electrical conduction system. The conduction system has numerous components that are responsible for the transmission of the electrical impulse that causes the contraction and recovery of the atria and ventricles. The *sinoatrial (SA) node*, considered to be the intrinsic pacemaker, normally is the initiator of rhythmic electrical impulses. It consists of a small amount of specialized muscle tissue and is located in the upper wall of the right atrium. Internodal pathways conduct the electrical impulse between the SA node and *AV node*, which is the location where the electrical impulse is slightly delayed before it passes into the ventricles. The *AV bundle* conducts the electrical impulse to the ventricles and it is divided into left and a right bundle branches. The bundle branches are further divided into *Purkinje fibers*, which transmit the impulse throughout the ventricles.

(G) The autonomic nervous system (ANS) is responsible for the rhythmicity and conduction properties of the myocardium. The atria have both sympathetic and parasympathetic fibers, while the ventricles have mostly sympathetic fibers. Sympathetic fibers increase the speed at which the SA node depolarizes, resulting in a faster heart rate. Parasympathetic fibers decrease the speed of SA node depolarization, which decreases heart rate. The normal range for resting heart rate is 60-100 beats/minute. *Bradycardia* is an abnormally slow heart (less than 60 beats/minute), and *tachycardia* is an abnormally fast heart rate, defined as greater than 100 beats/minute.

(H) An *electrocardiogram* (ECG) graphically represents the heart's electrical changes (recorded by electrodes on the skin) during the cardiac cycle. The cardiac cycle consists of several waves that represent depolarization and repolarization of the atria and ventricles. The first wave is the *P-wave*. This corresponds to atrial depolarization, which causes the contraction of the atria and the movement of blood down to the ventricles. The depolarization of the ventricles during the *QRS complex* (QRS complex consists of the *Q-wave*, *R-wave*, and *S-wave*) results in ventricular contraction, which produces the force to circulate blood through the pulmonary and peripheral blood vessels. The *T-wave* corresponds to ventricular repolarization, which can be thought of as the recovery from depolarization. The atria also repolarize, but this activity is masked on an EKG by the large QRS complex, which occurs simultaneously.

(I) Five major blood vessels manage blood flow to and from the heart: the superior and inferior venae cavae, the aorta, the pulmonary artery, and the pulmonary vein.

The superior vena cava is a large vein that drains blood from the head and upper body. The inferior vena cava is a large vein that drains blood from the lower body. The aorta is the largest artery in the human body and carries blood from the heart to body tissues. The pulmonary arteries carry blood from the heart to the lungs. The pulmonary veins transport blood from the lungs to the heart.

In the human body, there are two types of circulation: pulmonary circulation and systemic circulation. Pulmonary circulation supplies blood to the lungs. Deoxygenated blood enters the right atrium of the heart and is routed through the tricuspid valve into the right ventricle. Deoxygenated blood then travels from the right ventricle of the heart through the pulmonary valve and into the pulmonary arteries. The pulmonary arteries carry the deoxygenated blood to the lungs. In the lungs, oxygen is absorbed and carbon dioxide is released. The pulmonary veins carry oxygenated blood to the left atrium of the heart.

Systemic circulation supplies blood to all other parts of the body, except the lungs. Oxygenated blood flows from the left atrium of the heart through the mitral, or bicuspid, valve into the left ventricle of the heart. Oxygenated blood is then routed from the left ventricle of the heart through the aortic valve and into the aorta. The aorta delivers blood to the systemic arteries, which supply the body tissues. In the tissues, oxygen and nutrients are exchanged for carbon dioxide and other wastes. The deoxygenated blood along with carbon dioxide and wastes enter the systemic veins, where they are returned to the right atrium of the heart via the superior and inferior vena cava.

Questions 1-5: The sample passage has nine sections, A-I. Choose the correct heading for sections requested below from the list of headings provided.

```
i. Types of Circulation

ii. The Myocardium

iii. The Circulatory System

iv. Measuring the Electrical Activity of
the Heart

v. The Electrical Conduction System

vi. The Arteries

vii. Regulation of the Electrical Activity
of the Heart

viii. The Heartbeat

ix. The Cardiac Cycle

x. Blood

xi. Blood Vessels
```

Write the correct number i-ix in the space provided.

1. Section B _____

2. Section C _____

3. Section D _____

4. Section E _____

5. Section F _____

6. Section H _____

Questions 7-11: *Label the parts of the heart on the diagram below using words from the provided box. Write your answers in the spaces provided.*

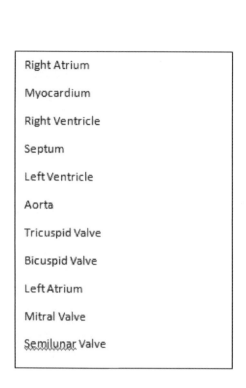

Right Atrium

Myocardium

Right Ventricle

Septum

Left Ventricle

Aorta

Tricuspid Valve

Bicuspid Valve

Left Atrium

Mitral Valve

Semilunar Valve

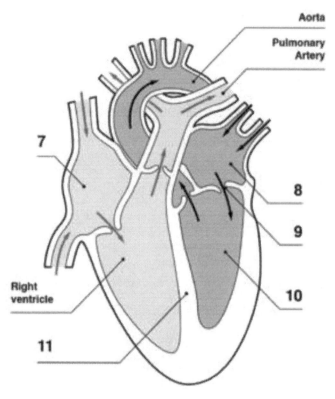

7. _____

8. _____

9. _____

10. _____

11. _____

12. Which of the following reflects the correct blood flow pathway (heart-valve-vessel)?
   a. Right atrium, left atrium, right ventricle, mitral valve, left ventricle, aorta
   b. Right atrium, tricuspid valve, right ventricle, left atrium, left ventricle, aorta
   c. Right atrium, right ventricle, left atrium, tricuspid valve, left ventricle, aorta
   d. Right atrium, right ventricle, pulmonary circulation, left atrium, mitral valve, left ventricle, aorta

13. Why do arteries have valves?
    a. They have valves to maintain high blood pressure so that capillaries diffuse nutrients properly.
    b. Their valves are designed to prevent backflow due to their low blood pressure.
    c. They have valves due to a leftover trait from evolution that, like the appendix, are useless.
    d. They do not have valves, but veins do.

14. What area of the heart is responsible for initiating rhythmic electrical impulses?
    a. Purkinje fibers
    b. Atrioventricular (AV) bundle
    c. Sinoatrial (SA) node
    d. Atrioventricular (AV) node

15. When reading an electrocardiogram, ventricular repolarization is associated with which graphical component?
    a. QRS complex
    b. P-wave
    c. T-wave
    d. PR segment

The following passage is from an introductory sociology textbook, discussing the demographic structure of a society. Read the passage and then answer the questions that follow.

Demography, or the study of human populations, involves a variety of closely related stimuli. First, economic factors play a significant role in the movement of people, as do climate, natural disasters, or internal unrest. For example, in recent years, millions of immigrants from the war-torn country of Syria, have moved as far as possible from danger. Many even risked their own lives in rickety boats on their way across the Mediterranean Sea. Although people are constantly moving, some consistencies remain throughout the world. First, people tend to live near reliable sources of food and water, which is why the first human civilizations sprung up in river valleys like the Indus River Valley in India, the Nile River Valley in Egypt, and the Yellow River Valley in Asia. Second, extreme temperatures tend to push people away, which is why the high latitudinal regions near the North and South Poles have such few inhabitants. Third, the vast majority of people tend to live in the Northern Hemisphere, due to the simple fact that more land lies in that part of the Earth. In keeping with these factors, human populations tend to be greater where human necessities are easily accessible, or at least are more readily available. In other words, such areas have a greater chance of having a higher population density than places without such characteristics.

Demographic patterns on Earth are not always stagnate. In contrast, people move and will continue to move as both push and pull factors fluctuate along with the flow of time. For example, in the 1940s, thousands of Europeans fled their homelands due to the impact of the Second World War. Today, thousands of migrants arrive on European shores each month due to conflicts in the Levant and difficult economic conditions in Northern Africa. Furthermore, as previously discussed, people tend to migrate to places with a greater economic benefit for themselves and their families. As a result, developed nations such as the United States, Germany, Canada, and Australia, have a net gain of migrants, while developing nations such as Somalia, Zambia, and Cambodia generally tend to see thousands of their citizens seek better lives elsewhere.

There are several key variables involved with changes in human population and its composition worldwide. Religion and religious conflict play a role in where people choose to live. For example, the

Nation of Israel won its independence in 1948 and has since attracted thousands of people of Jewish descent from all over the world. Additionally, the United States has long attracted people from all over the world, due to its promise of religious freedom inherent within its own Constitution. In contrast, nations like Saudi Arabia and Iran do not typically tolerate different religions, resulting in a decidedly uniform religious (and oftentimes ethnic) composition. Other factors such as economic opportunity, social unrest, and cost of living also play a vital role in demographic composition.

These such factors all can influence human migration, or the movement of people from one country to another. Migration is governed by two primary causes: *push factors*, which are reasons causing someone to leave an area, and *pull factors*, which are factors luring someone to a particular place. These two factors often work in concert with one another. For example, the United States of America has experienced significant *internal migration* from the industrial states in the Northeast (such as New York, New Jersey, Connecticut) to the Southern and Western states. This massive migration, which continues into the present-day, is due to high rents in the northeast, dreadfully cold winters, and lack of adequate retirement housing, all of which are push factors. These push factors lead to migration to the *sunbelt*, a term geographers use to describe states with warm climates and less intense winters.

In addition to internal migrations within nations or regions, international migration also takes place between countries, continents, and other regions. The United States has long been the world's leading nation in regard to *immigration*, the process of having people come into a nation's boundaries. Conversely, developing nations that suffer from high levels of poverty, pollution, warfare, and other violence all have significant push factors, which cause people to leave and move elsewhere. This process, known as *emigration*, is when people in a particular area leave in order to seek a better life in a different—usually better—location.

Patterns of migration are generally economically motivated. For example, the United States underwent a significant population shift from 1916-1930 due to its entrance into the First World War. Because of the war, thousands of factories opened and needed workers to produce munitions for the war effort. Answering the call of opportunity, thousands of African Americans, who had lived on farms since the cessation of the Civil War, packed up their belongings and moved to cities like Detroit, Los Angeles, Milwaukee, and Cleveland. This mass internal migration, which historians termed the *Great Migration*, is an excellent example of how economic forces work to stimulate human migration, thus drastically altering a nation's demographic patterns.

Demographic shifts—the apparent changes in the size, distribution, composition, and growth of a population—inevitably catalyze social changes as micro- and macro-communities expand disperse, shift, and contract. Demographic shifts influence human beings to respond in different ways. Demographic shifts can be the root of war, immigration, genocide, famine, and panic. Additionally, they can be the root of harmony, peace, stability, and social justice. Demography and sociology are so integrally linked that it is hard to disassociate the two fields.

In sociology, there are two major theories of demographic change: the Malthusian theory and the demographic transition theory. Created by English economist Thomas Malthus (1766-1834), Malthusian theory argues that if births and population increases burgeon in an unchecked fashion then a national, regional, or global community will outstrip its food supply. According to Mathus, who authored a book entitled *An Essay on the Principle of Population* (1789), food supplies increase arithmetically or linearly (1, 2, 3, 4, etc.) while population increase geometrically (2, 4, 8, 16, etc.). Inheritors of the Malthusian theory, frequently referred to as the New Malthusians, later developed the exponential growth curve, which states that population growth tends to double at near-equal intervals.

Detractors of Malthusian theory, traditionally called Anti-Malthusians, gravitate toward the so-called demographic transition theory. Demographic transition refers to a three-stage historical process of population growth: 1) high birth rates/high death rates, 2) high birth rates/low death rates, 3) low birth rates/low death rates. Some inheritors of this theory add a fourth stage: 4) deaths outnumber births.

The availability of resources affects the human population. Humans require basic resources such as food and water for survival, as well as additional resources for healthy lifestyles. Therefore, access to these resources helps determine the survival rate of humans. For much of human existence, economies have had limited ability to extract resources from the natural world, which restricted the growth rate of populations. However, the development of new technologies, combined with increasing demand for certain products, has pushed resource use to a new level. On the one hand, this led to higher living standards that ensured that fewer people would die. However, this has also brought mass population growth. Admittedly, countries with higher standards of living often have lower birthrates. Even so, the increasing exploitation of resources has sharply increased the world's population as a whole to unsustainable levels. The rising population leads, in turn, to more demand for resources that cannot be met. This creates poverty, reduced living conditions, and higher death rates. As a result, economics can significantly influence local and world population levels.

Technology is also intricately related to population, resources, and economics. The role of demand within economies has incentivized people to innovate new technologies that enable societies to have a higher quality of life and greater access to resources. Entrepreneurs expand technologies by finding ways to create new products for the market. The Industrial Revolution, in particular, illustrates the relationship between economics and technology because the ambitions of businessmen led to new infrastructure that enabled more efficient and sophisticated use of resources. Many of these inventions reduced the amount of work necessary for individuals and allowed the development of leisure activities, which, in turn, created new economic markets. However, economic systems can also limit the growth of technology. In the case of monopolies, the lack of alternative suppliers reduces the incentive to meet and exceed consumer expectations. Moreover, as demonstrated by the effects of economics on resources, technology's increasing ability to extract resources can lead to their depletion and create significant issues that need to be addressed.

A population's size can grow or decline based on fluctuating birth rates, death rates, immigration, and emigration. The *birth rate* is defined as the total number of live births per 1,000 individuals in a defined population in a year. The *death rate*, or *mortality rate*, is defined as the total number of deaths per 1,000 individuals in a defined population in a year. *Immigration* refers to a person or organism coming from another population to the one currently being examined, and *emigration* refers a person or organism leaving that population to settle elsewhere. Because these are the chief factors affecting a population's size, the rate of its growth can be determined from them.

Other variables such as food availability, adequate shelter, and water supply can also affect population. These resources are finite and help determine the carrying capacity of a particular geographic area. *Carrying capacity* is defined as the maximum number of individuals that can be sustained indefinitely in a particular habitat. As a population of humans grows, other factors such as government, education, economics, healthcare, and cultural values will also begin to influence the population.

As time goes on, certain countries may experience population growth while others experience its decline. Population growth, especially if unchecked, can be troubling when a community grows to a point that exceeds its carrying capacity.. Ultimately, levels of emigration may rise as individuals leave in search of more favorable conditions. Conversely, population decline can also be threatening due to the diminished pools of individuals available for labor and reproduction. Ultimately, rising levels of immigration will be needed to remedy this stress on the population.

The Demographic Transition Model (DTM) explains changes in two key areas, birth rate and death rate, and their effect on the total population of a country as it undergoes economic and industrial development. This model was introduced in 1929. Birth rate is defined as the number of live births per 1,000 individuals in a population over the course of an entire year, while death rate is defined as the total number of deaths per 1,000 individuals in a population over the course of an entire year.

As a general rule, a country will progress through stages as it undergoes economic and industrial development. Very few countries are in stage 1 of the model. Most of the developing countries are grouped in stage 2 or 3 of the model, while most of the industrialized countries are categorized in stage 3 or 4 of the model. The first stage of the Demographic Transition Model is termed the High Stationary phase. It is characterized by both a high birth and a high death rate. These factors combine to produce a constant, relatively low total population. High birth rates may be accounted for by factors such as poor family planning, high infant and child death rates, and child labor requirements for farming and manufacturing. High death rates may be accounted for by factors such as famine, poor sanitation, poor healthcare, and disease epidemics. Before the Industrial Revolution, most of the world's countries were categorized as stage 1. Today, only the least economically developed countries would be classified as this stage. The second stage is called the Early Expanding stage and it is characterized by a high birth rate and a rapidly decreasing death rate. These factors converge to produce a rapid increase in the total population. Rapidly decreasing death rates may be explained by falling infant and child death rates, improved sanitation, improvements in healthcare, and better nutrition. Today, the African countries of Ethiopia, Kenya, and Egypt are examples of countries classified in this stage. The Late Expanding stage is the name for the third stage of the DTM. It is characterized by a decreasing birth rate along with a continued falling (but less rapid) death rate. These factors continue to produce an increase in total population, but at a slower rate than seen in stage 2. Child welfare laws, a desire for smaller families, and the changing role of women in the workplace may explain the effect of falling birth rates on the total population. Current examples of countries grouped in this stage are Brazil, South Korea, and India. Lastly, in the fourth stage, the Low Stationary phase, both a low birth rate and death rate are seen. As a result, the factors combine to have a stabilizing effect on total population. Current examples of countries classified in this stage are the United States, Canada, and Great Britain.

16. All EXCEPT which of the following are true of an area with an extremely high population density?
    a. Competition for resources is intense
    b. Greater strain on public services exists
    c. Most are found in rural areas
    d. Most are found in urban areas

17. Which of the following could be considered a pull factor for a particular area?
    a. High rates of unemployment
    b. Low GDP
    c. Educational opportunity
    d. High population density

Questions 18-23: Match each statement with the stage of the Demographic Transition Model in which it occurs or is TRUE. Write the corresponding letter of the stage on the spaces provided. You may use each letter more than once or not at all.

18. Characterized by both a low birth rate and death rate _____

19. The factors of this stage interact in such a way as to have a stabilizing effect on the total population _____

20. Characterized by a high birth rate and a rapidly decreasing death rate _____

21. There is a constant, relatively low population _____

22. In current times, the least common or likely stage for a county _____

23. Examples of countries in this stage are Ethiopia and Egypt _____

| A. Stage 1 |
| B. Stage 2 |
| C. Stage 3 |
| D. Stage 4 |
| E. Stage 5 |

24. Reread the following sentences:

Demographic patterns on Earth are not always stagnate. In contrast, people move and will continue to move as both push and pull factors fluctuate along with the flow of time.

The word *stagnant* most nearly means:

    a. Predictable
    b. Changing
    c. Stationary
    d. Putrid

Questions 25-28: Complete the following table using the letters corresponding to the correct information in the box. You may use each letter more than once or not at all.

Pull Factor	25.
Push Factor	26.
Immigration	27.
Emigration	28.

A. Moving to the United States from Finland
B. Religious freedom
C. Cost of living
D. Religious intolerance
E. Leaving Ireland for Scotland

The following passage about the origins of the American Revolution and founding of the United States would be found in an introductory history textbook. Read the passage and then answer the questions that follow.

The French colonies in Canada threatened the British settlements. France and Britain had been enemies for centuries. Religious differences reinforced their hostility; the British were Protestant and the French were mostly Catholic. Far fewer colonists settled in "New France," but they often clashed with the British, especially over the lucrative fur trade. Both the British and French sought to dominate the trade in beaver pelts, which were used to make hats in Europe. The British and French fought a series of colonial wars between 1689 and 1748 that failed to resolve the struggle for dominance in North America.

Eventually, the contest culminated in the French and Indian War (also known as the Seven Years' War), which ended in 1763. The French initially enjoyed the upper hand because they were able to persuade more Native American tribes to support them. The Native Americans felt the French were less likely to encroach on their territory than the land-hungry British. The Native Americans launched devastating raids along the British colonial frontier. However, the British eventually emerged victorious after they blockaded the French colonies in Canada. This prevented the French from bringing in reinforcements or from resupplying their Native American allies with gunpowder and ammunition. Native American raids subsided and eventually the French surrendered almost all of their colonial possessions in North America. Some historians consider this war the first global conflict because battles were also fought in Europe, Asia, and Africa.

The French defeat radically altered the balance of power in North America. Previously, Native Americans had been able to play the French and British against each other, but now they were without many of their French allies. In addition, the French and Indian War also set the stage for the American Revolution. Although victorious, the British monarchy spent an enormous amount of money and the war doubled the national debt. In order to pay off the debts, King George III began imposing taxes upon the North American colonies, which eventually led to revolution.

Since 1651, the British crown had tried to control trade within its empire, which eventually led to tension and discontent in the North American colonies. That year, the monarchy introduced the Navigation Acts, which prevented the North American colonies from trading directly with other European powers—all goods had to be shipped to Britain first. This was an attempt to keep wealth within the British Empire and to prevent other empires from profiting from their colonies. This was an example of mercantilism—an economic policy that formed the foundation of Britain's empire. Mercantilism called for government regulation in the form of tariffs, a tax on imports from other countries. This raised prices on foreign goods and encouraged British imperial subjects to purchase goods made in Britain or the colonies. This reduced imports and maximized exports, thus enriching the British Empire.

The Molasses Act in 1731 was another outgrowth of mercantilism. This law imposed a higher tax on the molasses that colonists purchased from the Dutch, French, or Spanish colonies. The tax was unpopular with the colonists and British imperial officials eventually decided not to enforce the tax. The Molasses Act had threatened to disrupt the pattern of triangular trade that had emerged in the Atlantic world. First, ships from Britain's North American colonies carried rum to Africa where it was traded for slaves and gold. Then, the ships took the slaves to French and Spanish colonies in the Caribbean and exchanged them for sugar or molasses. In the last part of the triangular trade system, merchants sailed back to North America where the sugar and molasses was used to make rum, and the cycle could start over again.

In addition to economic connections, many other bonds also bridged the Atlantic Ocean. Most colonists shared a common language, common religion, and common culture. However, as the colonies grew in population, they began to develop local institutions and a separate sense of identity. For example, it became common for ministers to receive their education at seminaries in North America rather than Britain. Newspapers also began to focus on printing more local news as well. Perhaps most importantly, the colonies began to exercise more control over their own political affairs. The British government retained control over international issues, such as war and trade, but the colonists controlled their own domestic affairs. Colonies began to form their own political assemblies and elect landowners who represented local districts. In addition, communications between the colonies and Britain were very slow because it took months for a ship to cross the Atlantic and return with a response.

A number of political acts by the British monarchy also led to more discontent among the colonies. After the French and Indian War ended in 1763, the king declared that the colonists could not settle west of the Appalachian Mountains. This was known as the Proclamation of 1763. Many colonists were frustrated because they had expected this territory would be open for expansion after the French had been defeated.

Additionally, taxes were imposed in an effort to help reduce the debt Britain amassed during the French and Indian War. In 1764, Parliament passed the Sugar Act, which reduced the tax on molasses but also provided for greater enforcement powers. Some colonists protested by organizing boycotts on British goods. One year later, in 1765, Parliament passed the Quartering Act, which required colonists to provide housing and food to British troops. This law was also very unpopular and led to protests in the North American colonies.

The Stamp Act of 1765 required the colonists to pay a tax on legal documents, newspapers, magazines and other printed materials. Colonial assemblies protested the tax and petitioned the British government in order to have it repealed. Merchants also organized boycotts and established correspondence committees in order to share information. Eventually, Parliament repealed the Stamp Act but simultaneously reaffirmed the Crown's right to tax the colonies.

In 1767, Parliament introduced the Townshend Acts, which imposed a tax on goods the colonies imported from Britain, such as tea, lead, paint, glass, and paper. The colonies protested again and British imperial officials were assaulted in some cases. The British government sent additional troops to North America to restore order. The arrival of troops in Boston only led to more tension that eventually culminated in the Boston Massacre in 1770, where five colonists were killed and eight were wounded. Except for the duty on tea, most of Townshend Act taxes were repealed after the Boston Massacre.

Parliament passed the Tea Act in 1773 and, although it actually reduced the tax on tea, it was another unpopular piece of legislation. The Tea Act allowed the British East India Company to sell its products directly, effectively cutting out colonial merchants and stirring more Anglo-American anger and resentment. This resulted in the Boston Tea Party in 1773, an incident in which colonial tea merchants disguised themselves as Indians before storming several British ships that were anchored in Boston harbor. Once aboard, the disguised colonists dumped more than 300 chests of tea into the water.

Because the British government was unable to identify the perpetrators, Parliament passed a series of laws that punished the entire colony of Massachusetts. These acts were known as the Coercive or Intolerable Acts. The first law closed the port of Boston until the tea had been paid for (an estimated $1.7 million in today's currency). The second act curtailed the authority of Massachusetts' colonial government. Instead of being elected by colonists, most government officials were now appointed by the king. In addition, the act restricted town meetings, the basic form of government in Massachusetts, and limited most villages to one meeting per year. This act angered colonists throughout the thirteen colonies because they feared their rights could be stripped away as well. A third act allowed for British soldiers to be tried in Britain if they were accused of a crime. The fourth act once again required colonists to provide food and shelter to British soldiers.

Colonists responded by forming the First Continental Congress in 1774, and all the colonies except for Georgia sent delegates. The delegates sought a compromise with the British government instead of launching an armed revolt. The First Continental Congress sent a petition to King George III affirming their loyalty but demanding the repeal of the Intolerable Acts. The delegates organized a boycott of imports from and exports to Britain until their demands were met.

The colonists began to form militias and gather weapons and ammunition. The first battle of the revolution began at Lexington and Concord in April 1775 when British troops tried to seize a supply of gunpowder and were confronted by about eighty Minutemen. A brief skirmish left eight colonists dead and ten wounded. Colonial reinforcements poured in and harassed the British force as they retreated to Boston. Although the battle did not result in many casualties, it marked the beginning of war.

A month later, the Second Continental Congress convened in Philadelphia. The delegates formed an army and appointed George Washington as commander in chief. Delegates were still reluctant to repudiate their allegiance to King George III and did not do so until they issued the Declaration of Independence on July 4, 1776. The Declaration drew on the ideas of the Enlightenment and declared that the colonists had the right to life, liberty, and the pursuit of happiness. The Declaration stated that the colonists had to break away from Britain because King George III had violated their rights.

After the Battle of Lexington and Concord, British troops retreated to Boston and the colonial militias laid siege to the city. Colonists built fortifications on Bunker Hill outside the city and British troops attacked the position in June 1775. The colonists inflicted heavy casualties on the British and killed a number of officers. However, the defenders ran out of ammunition and British troops captured Bunker Hill on the third assault. Although it was a defeat for the colonists, the Battle of Bunker Hill demonstrated that they could stand and fight against the disciplined and professional British army.

The British army initially had the upper hand and defeated colonial forces in a number of engagements. The Americans did not achieve a victory until the Battle of Trenton in December 1776. Washington famously crossed the Delaware River on Christmas Day and launched a surprise attack against Hessian mercenaries. They captured more than 1,000 soldiers and suffered very minimal casualties. The victory at Trenton bolstered American morale and showed that they could defeat professional European soldiers.

The Battle of Saratoga in New York in the fall of 1777 was an important turning point in the American War for Independence. American troops surrounded and captured more than 6,000 British soldiers. This victory convinced the French king to support the revolutionaries by sending troops, money, weapons, and ships to the American continent. French officers who fought alongside the Patriots brought back many ideas with them that eventually sparked a revolution in France in 1789.

French support was very important in the last major battle of the revolution at Yorktown, Virginia, in 1781. American troops laid siege to General Cornwallis's British forces at Yorktown. The French fleet defeated a British naval squadron sent to relieve Cornwallis. French and American troops began attacking the British fortifications in Yorktown; a sustained artillery bombardment by American guns eventually forced Cornwallis to surrender. This ended the Revolutionary War, and in 1783 the British signed the Treaty of Paris. Britain recognized the United States as an independent country and set the Mississippi River as the nation's western border. However, British troops continued to occupy several forts in the Great Lakes region.

In addition, tens of thousands of colonists who remained loyal to the British Empire fled the United States after the war. They were known as loyalists and many thousands had joined militias and fought against the patriots. Some loyalists fled to Canada or Britain but many remained in the United States. Many Native American tribes had sided with the British as well in an attempt to curb western expansion. No Native American leaders signed the Treaty of Paris and they refused to give up their territories, which led to further conflict as the new American nation began to expand westward.

Questions 29-40: *Fill out the provided flow chart with important events leading up to and involving the American Revolution in chronological order. Write the letter of the correct answer from the answer bank in the numbered box. Each letter will be used exactly ONE time.*

Flow Chart	Answer Bank
Molasses Act	A. Boston Tea Party
↓	B. First Continental Congress
29.	C. French and Indian War Ends
↓	D. Battle of Trenton
30.	E. The Sugar Act
↓	F. Declaration of Independence
31.	G. Townshend Acts
↓	H. The Stamp Act
32.	I. Boston Massacre
↓	J. Treaty of Paris
33.	K. Battle at Lexington and Concord
↓	L. Battle of Saratoga
34.	
↓	
35.	
↓	
36.	

↓

37.

↓

38.

↓

39.

↓

40.

Answer Explanations

1. xi

2. x

3. ii

4. ix

5. v

6. iv

7. Right Atrium

8. Left Atrium

9. Mitral Valve

10. Left Ventricle

11. Septum

12. D: Blood returning to the heart from the body enters the right atrium and then moves through the tricuspid valve into the right ventricle. After filling, the right ventricle contracts, and the tricuspid valve closes, pushing blood through the pulmonary semilunar valve into the pulmonary arteries for pulmonary circulation, after which it enters the left atrium. Contraction of the left atrium moves blood through the bicuspid valve into the left ventricle (the largest heart chamber). When the bicuspid valve closes and the left ventricle contracts, blood is forced into the aortic valve through the aorta and on to systemic circulation.

13. D: Veins have valves, but arteries do not. Valves in veins are designed to prevent backflow, since they are the furthest blood vessels from the pumping action of the heart and steadily increase in volume (which decreases the available pressure). Capillaries diffuse nutrients properly because of their thin walls and high surface area and are not particularly dependent on positive pressure.

14. C: The sinoatrial (SA) node is the initiator of the rhythmic electrical impulses of the cardiac cycle. The SA node is located in the upper wall of the right atrium and contains a small locus of specialized muscle fibers that naturally generate action potentials.

15. C: On an EKG, the T-wave corresponds to the recovery of the ventricles from depolarization, which is also known as repolarization. On the reading, this occurs after the QRS complex – the graphical representation of ventricular depolarization and contraction.

16. C: Population density, which is the total number of people divided by the total land area, generally tends to be much higher in urban areas than rural ones. This is true due to high-rise apartment complexes, sewage and freshwater infrastructure, and complex transportation systems, allowing for easy movement of food from nearby farms. Consequently, competition among citizens for resources is certainly higher in high-density areas, as are greater strains on infrastructure within urban centers.

17. C: Pull factors are reasons people immigrate to a particular area. Obviously, educational opportunities attract thousands of people on a global level and on a local level. For example, generally, areas with strong schools have higher property values, due to the relative demand for housing in those districts. The same is true for nations with better educational opportunities. Unemployment, low GDP, and incredibly high population densities may serve to deter people from moving to a certain place, and can be considered push factors.

18. D

19. D

20. B

21. A

22. A

23. B

24. C

25. B

26. D

27. A

28. E

29. C: French and Indian War Ends, 1763

30. E: The Sugar Act, 1764

31. H: The Stamp Act, 1765

32. G: Townshend Acts, 1767

33. I: Boston Massacre, 1770

34. A: Boston Tea Party, 1773

35. B: First Continental Congress, 1774

36. K: Battle at Lexington and Concord, 1775

37. F: Declaration of Independence, July of 1776

38. D: Battle of Trenton, December of 1776

39. L: Battle of Saratoga, 1777

40. J: Treaty of Paris, 1783

General Training Reading Practice Questions

The following train timetable should be used for questions 1-5.

Departs	From	To	Arrives	Duration	Changes
8:41	Whitestone Platform 1	Paddington Platform 3	9:56	1h 15m	1
8:58	Whitestone Platform 1	Greensboro Platform 1	9:56	58m	0
9:07	Whitestone Platform 3	Paddington Platform 2	10:31	1h 24m	1
9:19	Whitestone Platform 1	Paddington Platform 4	10:23	1h 4m	0
9:56	Whitestone Platform 3	Greensboro Platform 1	11:23	1h 27m	2

Question 1-5: Fill in the blanks using the table above. Write NO MORE THAN the words or numbers that fill a SINGLE box from the train table.

1. The fastest train that goes to Paddington departs at _____.

2. A rider who wants to arrive in Paddington on Platform 2 should catch the train from _____.

3. The train ride that is 1hr 24min departs at _____.

4. If someone needs to arrive in Paddington by 10:30, he or she should take the train that leaves at _____.

5. The train that leaves at 9:07, has _____ change(s).

The following listing was posted in the "Rooms and Shares Available" section of an online community marketplace. Read the listing and then answer the questions that follow.

Suite of rooms available for rent in downtown Easthampton - $700/month

We have a large house and we aren't using much of the space. It would be perfect for a student or someone seeking summer housing. We are open to continuing the arrangement beyond the summer, but if you just want to do summer, that works too.

About us: mid 20's married couple with a sweet dog. One is a full-time student who commutes every day and the other is a working professional. We both have extremely long days so we aren't home much.

The house: located in the center of town. Right on the bus line, very close to the library, YMCA, grocery store, etc. We have a good sized fenced-in yard and a garden with raspberries several vegetables, as long as the weather cooperates!

Your space in the house: Upstairs in the house, half of the rooms close off completely in their own wing. This is your space. There are three rooms: a large room (16x16) that you could turn into a living room, an office or smaller bedroom (10x12), and the master bedroom (20x10). You would use the bathroom and kitchen downstairs (there is a toilet but no shower upstairs). We have laundry facilities in the basement that you can use in the evenings. We have a deck and a nice yard big yard and we are on a quiet street, even though it is right in the center of town.

Please ask any questions or if you would like to see pictures or come over and take a look. All we ask is that whomever is interested does not smoke and is respectful of our fairly quiet house. If you do have a car, there is plenty of parking right in our driveway.

Rent is $700 a month and includes all utilities except Internet and cable. This is an additional $40/month if you want to join our package. To move in, you need first month's rent, a $500 security deposit, and the names and numbers of two references we can call on your behalf.

Thank you!

Questions 6-16: The following table is a checklist made by a potential tenant to take notes as she searches listings. Complete the table using the information in the ad. Write 'YES' if the information is given in the ad and permitted or present in the rental, 'NO' if it is given in the ad but not permitted or present, and 'NO MENTION' if the information is not present in the ad.

6. Total cost to move in less than $1200	
7. Laundry use	
8. Number of pets allowed	
9. At least 3 rooms available	
10. Any prohibited activities	
11. Home gym	
12. Current tenants are all professionals	
13. Garden with strawberries	
14. Looking for female tenants only	
15. Close to the shopping center	
16. Monthly rent with Internet less than $720	

Read the following cover letter and then answer the questions that follow.

To Whom It May Concern:

I'm writing in regards to the Writer/Producer position at Shadow Heat. I graduated with my MA degree in English at the University of Texas in May 2016 where I taught technical writing and writing arguments for my fellowship. My years taking and teaching English courses have enabled me to develop strong writing skills, which I believe will contribute greatly to the position in question.

Although a work in progress, my website, attached below, features technical writing, graphic design, blog writing, and creative writing samples. My passion for writing in order to connect with a specific audience is demonstrated by my various publications as well as my degrees that focus heavily on academic and creative writing. I would love to write for your company and hope you'll consider me for this position.

I'm highly motivated, carrying energy and creativity to my work. My nine years' experience in higher education enables me to adapt to changing ideals and trends while also maintaining personal values. I hope that you'll consider me for this position. I look forward to hearing from you!

Thanks!

17. What type of writing does this passage sound like?
    a. A how-to document on teaching
    b. A consumer email to a corporation

c. A letter of interest for a job

d. A memo concerning employees in the workplace

18. Which of the following is correct information?
    a. The writer of the letter is a writer/producer at Shadow Heat.
    b. The writer of the letter has a Master's degree in English.
    c. The writer of the letter has ten years' experience in higher education.
    d. The writer of the letter is applying to be a website designer.

19. The writer of the letter has experience with which of the following? Select all the apply.
    a. Working at Shadow Heat
    b. Blog writing
    c. Technical writing
    d. Teaching graphic design
    e. Publishing writing
    f. Changing trends

20. Which of the following people would most likely be the intended recipient of the letter?
    a. A job candidate looking for work as a writer
    b. A job candidate looking for a job at Shadow Heat
    c. An employee at Shadow Heat
    d. The hiring manager at Shadow Heat

21. Which additional piece of information from the letter writer would be most useful for the recipient of the letter?
    a. A resume
    b. A professional headshot
    c. A job description for the desired position
    d. Shadow Heat's business card

Read the following job description and then answer the questions that follow.

University of Greenwich
Alumni Relations and Development Office
Prospect Research Assistant- Job Description

Job Description: The Prospect Research Assistant position provides data support to the University by receiving, reviewing, researching, and entering data into the University's fundraising database in accordance with established procedures. There is also opportunity to work at events including Alumni Weekend and Commencement and to assist with general office duties.

Duties & Responsibilities:
- Updates fundraising database with information compiled from research products produced by Prospect Research.

- Enters constituent data by following data policies and procedures.

- Maintains high level of accuracy, consistency and integrity of data and ensures information is input into database in a timely manner.

- Researches and updates donor records in response to information received through the Research Request box and social media vehicles.

- Reviews news alerts for alumni-related updates and suggests recommendations of alumni to be featured in University publications and social media.

- Proofreads research documents.

- Assists in basic research as required.

- Contributes to a team effort and performs other duties as needed such as compiling, copying, filing, and sorting.

- Performs other duties as assigned.

Desired Qualifications: We are seeking someone with strong skills in attention to detail, confidentiality, thoroughness, data entry, organization, and analyzing information. He or she should be professional and positive, results driven, trustworthy, and possess the ability to work independently.

The candidate must be available to work 4-8 hours per week within the hours of 9:00am-5:00pm Monday through Friday. We are happy to offer a flexible work schedule around a student's class schedule.

He or she must be able to travel to 24 Willow Street but an on-campus shuttle service is available to and from our office.

22. This sample would most likely be composed by which of the following people?
    a. A job candidate
    b. A research assistant
    c. A manager at the University of Greenwich
    d. A fundraiser

Questions 23-27: Complete the following sentences using NO MORE THAN 3 words.

23. Job candidates without cars can reach the office by way of the _____.

24. The employee will update donor records in response to information received through social media outlets and the _____.

25. The employee may assist at events like Alumni Weekend and _____.

26. The University maintains a _____ database.

27. The job schedule can be worked around a _____.

Questions 28-30 are based on the following passage:

Smoking is Terrible
Smoking tobacco products is terribly destructive. A single cigarette contains over 4,000 chemicals, including 43 known carcinogens and 400 deadly toxins. Some of the most dangerous ingredients include tar, carbon monoxide, formaldehyde, ammonia, arsenic, and DDT. Smoking can cause numerous types

of cancer including throat, mouth, nasal cavity, esophagus, stomach, pancreas, kidney, bladder, and cervical.

Cigarettes contain a drug called nicotine, one of the most addictive substances known to man. Addiction is defined as a compulsion to seek the substance despite negative consequences. According to the National Institute of Drug Abuse, nearly 35 million smokers expressed a desire to quit smoking in 2015; however, more than 85 percent of those addicts will not achieve their goal. Almost all smokers regret picking up that first cigarette. You would be wise to learn from their mistake if you have not yet started smoking.

According to the U.S. Department of Health and Human Services, 16 million people in the United States presently suffer from a smoking-related condition and nearly nine million suffer from a serious smoking-related illness. According to the Centers for Disease Control and Prevention (CDC), tobacco products cause nearly six million deaths per year. This number is projected to rise to over eight million deaths by 2030. Smokers, on average, die ten years earlier than their nonsmoking peers.

In the United States, local, state, and federal governments typically tax tobacco products, which leads to high prices. Nicotine addicts sometimes pay more for a pack of cigarettes than for a few gallons of gas. Additionally, smokers tend to stink. The smell of smoke is all-consuming and creates a pervasive nastiness. Smokers also risk staining their teeth and fingers with yellow residue from the tar.

Smoking is deadly, expensive, and socially unappealing. Clearly, smoking is not worth the risks.

28. Which of the following statements most accurately summarizes the passage?
    a. Tobacco is less healthy than many alternatives.
    b. Tobacco is deadly, expensive, and socially unappealing, and smokers would be much better off kicking the addiction.
    c. In the United States, local, state, and federal governments typically tax tobacco products, which leads to high prices.
    d. Tobacco products shorten smokers' lives by ten years and kill more than six million people per year.

29. The author would be most likely to agree with which of the following statements?
    a. Smokers should only quit cold turkey and avoid all nicotine cessation devices.
    b. Other substances are more addictive than tobacco.
    c. Smokers should quit for whatever reason that gets them to stop smoking.
    d. People who want to continue smoking should advocate for a reduction in tobacco product taxes.

30. Which of the following represents an opinion statement on the part of the author?
    a. According to the Centers for Disease Control and Prevention (CDC), tobacco products cause nearly six million deaths per year.
    b. Nicotine addicts sometimes pay more for a pack of cigarettes than a few gallons of gas.
    c. They also risk staining their teeth and fingers with yellow residue from the tar.
    d. Additionally, smokers tend to stink. The smell of smoke is all-consuming and creates a pervasive nastiness.

Questions 31-35: Complete the following summary using NO MORE THAN 1 WORD per answer.

Nicotine is a/an 31. _____substance found in 32. _____. Throat, mouth, and esophagus are among the many types of 33. _____ that smoking can cause. Nearly six million deaths annually are caused by 34. _____ products. Smoking can shorten one's 35. _____.

Questions 36-40 are based upon the following passage:

This excerpt is adaptation from Charles Dickens' speech in Birmingham in England on December 30, 1853 on behalf of the Birmingham and Midland Institute.

My Good Friends,—When I first imparted to the committee of the projected Institute my particular wish that on one of the evenings of my readings here the main body of my audience should be composed of working men and their families, I was animated by two desires; first, by the wish to have the great pleasure of meeting you face to face at this Christmas time, and accompany you myself through one of my little Christmas books; and second, by the wish to have an opportunity of stating publicly in your presence, and in the presence of the committee, my earnest hope that the Institute will, from the beginning, recognise one great principle—strong in reason and justice—which I believe to be essential to the very life of such an Institution. It is, that the working man shall, from the first unto the last, have a share in the management of an Institution which is designed for his benefit, and which calls itself by his name.

I have no fear here of being misunderstood—of being supposed to mean too much in this. If there ever was a time when any one class could of itself do much for its own good, and for the welfare of society—which I greatly doubt—that time is unquestionably past. It is in the fusion of different classes, without confusion; in the bringing together of employers and employed; in the creating of a better common understanding among those whose interests are identical, who depend upon each other, who are vitally essential to each other, and who never can be in unnatural antagonism without deplorable results, that one of the chief principles of a Mechanics' Institution should consist. In this world a great deal of the bitterness among us arises from an imperfect understanding of one another. Erect in Birmingham a great Educational Institution, properly educational; educational of the feelings as well as of the reason; to which all orders of Birmingham men contribute; in which all orders of Birmingham men meet; wherein all orders of Birmingham men are faithfully represented—and you will erect a Temple of Concord here which will be a model edifice to the whole of England.

Contemplating as I do the existence of the Artisans' Committee, which not long ago considered the establishment of the Institute so sensibly, and supported it so heartily, I earnestly entreat the gentlemen—earnest I know in the good work, and who are now among us,—by all means to avoid the great shortcoming of similar institutions; and in asking the working man for his confidence, to set him the great example and give him theirs in return. You will judge for yourselves if I promise too much for the working man, when I say that he will stand by such an enterprise with the utmost of his patience, his perseverance, sense, and support; that I am sure he will need no charitable aid or condescending patronage; but will readily and cheerfully pay for the advantages which it confers; that he will prepare himself in individual cases where he feels that the adverse circumstances around him have rendered it necessary; in a word, that he will feel his

responsibility like an honest man, and will most honestly and manfully discharge it. I
now proceed to the pleasant task to which I assure you I have looked forward for a long

36. Which term is most closely aligned with the definition of the term *working man* as it is defined in the
following passage?

> You will judge for yourselves if I promise too much for the working man, when I say that he will
> stand by such an enterprise with the utmost of his patience, his perseverance, sense, and
> support . . .

  a. Plebian
  b. Viscount
  c. Entrepreneur
  d. Bourgeois

37. Which of the following statements most closely correlates with the definition of the term
working man as it is defined in Question 26?
  a. A working man is not someone who works for institutions or corporations, but someone who is
  well versed in the workings of the soul.
  b. A working man is someone who is probably not involved in social activities because the physical
  demand for work is too high.
  c. A working man is someone who works for wages among the middle class.
  d. The working man has historically taken to the field, to the factory, and now to the screen.

38. Based upon the contextual evidence provided in the passage above, what is the meaning of the term
enterprise in the third paragraph?
  a. Company
  b. Courage
  c. Game
  d. Cause

39. The speaker addresses his audience as *My Good Friends*—what kind of credibility does this
salutation give to the speaker?
  a. The speaker is an employer addressing his employees, so the salutation is a way for the boss to
  bridge the gap between himself and his employees.
  b. The speaker's salutation is one from an entertainer to his audience, and uses the friendly
  language to connect to his audience before a serious speech.
  c. The salutation gives the serious speech that follows a somber tone, as it is used ironically.
  d. The speech is one from a politician to the public, so the salutation is used to grab the audience's
  attention.

40. According to the aforementioned passage, what is the speaker's second desire for his time in front
of the audience?
  a. To read a Christmas story
  b. For the working man to have a say in his institution which is designed for his benefit.
  c. To have an opportunity to stand in their presence
  d. For the life of the institution to be essential to the audience as a whole

Answer Explanations

1. 9:19

2. Whitestone Platform 3

3. 9:07

4. 8:41

5. 1

6. NO

7. YES

8. NO MENTION

9. YES

10. YES

11. NO MENTION

12. NO

13. NO

14. NO MENTION

15. NO MENTION

16. NO

17. C: This is a letter of interest or cover letter for a job position. It would likely accompany a resume and job application and be written by a job candidate interested in an available position. It does not explain the process or the "how-to" for anything, so Choice *A* is incorrect. Choices *B* and *D* are also incorrect because it is not written by a consumer of a product nor does it concern a workplace's employees.

18. B: The letter writer says: "I graduated with my MA degree in English at the University of Texas in May 2016 where I taught technical writing and writing arguments for my fellowship." MA is the abbreviation for Master of Arts, which is a Master's Degree. The other choices are inaccurate or not mentioned in the letter.

19. B & C: The letter writer is an experienced creative and technical writer with experience in "technical writing, graphic design, blog writing, and creative writing.' Choice *A* is incorrect because the person wants to work at Shadow Heat but does not yet have a position there, so he or she does not have experience working there. Choice *D* is incorrect because the writer has experience teaching English, not graphic design; he or she has experience with graphic design, but did not mention teaching it. Choices *E* and *F* are also incorrect. Publishing writing is not a skill mentioned and the writer doesn't have experience *changing* trends, but can adapt well to changes in trends, demonstrating flexibility.

20. D: This is a cover letter that would accompany a job application for a position at Shadow Heat. Therefore, it is written by an interested job candidate looking to become an employee at Shadow Heat and is intended for the employer or the hiring manager at Shadow Heat, which is Choice *D.* The other choices are ways to describe the letter writer.

21. A: A resume would support the letter writer's application as he or she is a job candidate for an open position. A resume would detail his or her education background, career experience, and related skills and would support the narrative presentation of this information in the letter. Choice *B,* a headshot, may accompany a resume or job application for some positions, it is not particularly relevant for a writer, and therefore, is not the best choice. Choices *C* and *D* are pieces of information that the recipient of the letter (the employer) may create or have, not the letter writer.

22. C: The provided passage is a job description for a research assistant position in the University of Greenwich's Alumni Relations and Development Office. Therefore, the person who wrote the position would be the employer, or Choice *C,* a manager at the University because he or she has the position to offer and is seeking a qualified candidate. All of the other choices are likely the intended audience for the job description or potential applicants for the position.

23. On-campus shuttle

24. Research Request Box

25. Commencement

26. Fundraising

27. Student's class schedule

28. B: The author is clearly opposed to tobacco. He cites disease and deaths associated with smoking. He points to the monetary expense and aesthetic costs. Choice *A* is wrong because alternatives to smoking are not even addressed in the passage. Choice *C* is wrong because it does not summarize the passage but rather is just a premise. Choice *D* is wrong because, while these statistics are a premise in the argument, they do not represent a summary of the piece. Choice *C* is the correct answer because it states the three critiques offered against tobacco and expresses the author's conclusion.

29. C: We are looking for something the author would agree with, so it will almost certainly be anti-smoking or an argument in favor of quitting smoking. Choice *A* is wrong because the author does not speak against means of cessation. Choice *B* is wrong because the author does not reference other substances, but does speak of how addictive nicotine, a drug in tobacco, is. Choice *D* is wrong because the author certainly would not encourage reducing taxes to encourage a reduction of smoking costs, thereby helping smokers to continue the habit. Choice *C* is correct because the author is definitely attempting to persuade smokers to quit smoking.

30. D: Here, we are looking for an opinion of the author's rather than a fact or statistic. Choice *A* is wrong because quoting statistics from the Centers of Disease Control and Prevention is stating facts, not opinions. Choice B is wrong because it expresses the fact that cigarettes sometimes cost more than a few gallons of gas. It would be an opinion if the author said that cigarettes were not affordable. Choice C is incorrect because yellow stains are a known possible adverse effect of smoking. Choice D is correct as an opinion because smell is subjective. Some people might like the smell of smoke, they might not have working olfactory senses, and/or some people might not find the smell of smoke akin to "pervasive nastiness," so this is the expression of an opinion. Thus, Choice D is the correct answer.

31. Addictive

32. Cigarettes

33. Cancers

34. Tobacco

35. Lifespan

36. D: *Working man* is most closely aligned with Choice D, *bourgeois.* In the context of the speech, the word *bourgeois* means *working* or *middle class.* Choice A, *plebian,* does suggest *common people;* however, this is a term that is specific to ancient Rome. Choice B, *viscount,* is a European title used to describe a specific degree of nobility. Choice C, *entrepreneur,* is a person who operates their own business.

37. C: In the context of the speech, the term *working man* most closely correlates with Choice C, *working man is someone who works for wages among the middle class.* Choice A is not mentioned in the passage and is off-topic. Choice B may be true in some cases, but it does not reflect the sentiment described for the term *working man* in the passage. Choice D may also be arguably true. However, it is not given as a definition but as *acts* of the working man, and the topics of *field, factory,* and *screen* are not mentioned in the passage.

38. D: *Enterprise* most closely means *cause.* Choices A, B, and C are all related to the term *enterprise.* However, Dickens speaks of a *cause* here, not a company, courage, or a game. *He will stand by such an enterprise* is a call to stand by a cause to enable the working man to have a certain autonomy over his own economic standing. The very first paragraph ends with the statement that the working man *shall . . . have a share in the management of an institution which is designed for his benefit.*

39. B: The speaker's salutation is one from an entertainer to his audience, and uses the friendly language to connect to his audience before a serious speech. Recall in the first paragraph that the speaker is there to "accompany [the audience] . . . through one of my little Christmas books," making him an author there to entertain the crowd with his own writing. The speech preceding the reading is the passage itself, and, as the tone indicates, a serious speech addressing the "working man." Although the passage speaks of employers and employees, the speaker himself is not an employer of the audience, so Choice A is incorrect. Choice C is also incorrect, as the salutation is not used ironically, but sincerely, as the speech addresses the wellbeing of the crowd. Choice D is incorrect because the speech is not given by a politician, but by a writer.

40. B: For the working man to have a say in his institution which is designed for his benefit. Choice *A* is incorrect because that is the speaker's *first* desire, not his second. Choices *C* and *D* are tricky because the language of both of these is mentioned after the word *second*. However, the speaker doesn't get to the second wish until the next sentence. Choices *C* and *D* are merely prepositions preparing for the statement of the main clause, Choice *B*.

Writing

The IELTS™ Writing section lasts 60 minutes and contains two tasks, both of which must be completed. On the Academic Test, the first task asks test takers to use a formal style of writing to explain or summarize a provided diagram, graph, table, or chart pertaining to data, the stages of a process, or the mechanics of an object or an event. It is expected that test takers write at least 150 words in about 20 minutes and that they describe the visual in their own words. In the second task, test takers are given a point of view or problem and must write a formal essay of 250 words in response. To do so, they are given about 40 minutes. Answers must be recorded on the answer sheet and must use complete sentences. Answers that are shorter than the stated lengths will be penalized. Longer responses are permitted so long as they are completed within the timeframe and remain on topic; points are deducted for answers that deviate from the question or topic.

On the General Training test, the first task asks test takers to write a personal or formal letter explaining a certain situation or requesting clarification or information. The topics for the letter writing task are everyday ones such as a letter to an employer justifying the request for a raise, one to a landlord to complain about issues with the maintenance department, or a letter to the local newspaper about an upcoming event in the planning stages. The instructions will have bullet points to inform test takers about the specific information they must include in the letter. Test takers can expect to make some sort of complaint, express an opinion or desire, explain a situation in detail, provide suggestions, and/or ask for or give factual information in the letter writing task. Another important consideration in the planning and writing stages is the style of writing that the writer will use to communicate their message. This will depend on the particular assignment they are given: who is their audience, how well they are supposed to know the recipient, and the purpose for the letter. For example, a more formal style should be employed when writing to a manager, whereas a personal or informal style is more appropriate when writing to an aunt or friend. Like the Academic Test, for the second task, test takers are given a point of view or problem and must write an essay in response, but it can be more personal in style and the topics are more general interest like the pros and cons of intergenerational households, whether children should get "screen time" (television, tablets, etc.), if sugary beverages should be taxed, solutions to landfill and trash problems, and how to enforce traffic laws like seatbelt use and no texting while driving.

Both tasks on both tests require test takers to carefully and fully read all provided instructions with the assignment to ensure that all relevant points are covered. Examiners are looking for responses to not only be of sufficient length (150 words for Task 1 and 250 for Task 2), but that writers stay on topic, organize ideas clearly and coherently, support their argument or opinion with facts and examples, and can communicate their ideas in a logical order, using a range of vocabulary and sentence structures with complex ideas, compelling writing, and a command of the English language. It should be noted that the response for Task 2 is expected to demonstrate more advanced grammar and vocabulary, more abstract ideas, and employ strong evidence and justification of ideas. Resultantly, Task 2 carries twice as much weight in scoring as Task 1 for the test taker's overall Writing Section score.

Written responses are evaluated on the following criteria:

- Task achievement/response: The strength and adherence to the assignment instructions, the degree to which one explains their thoughts or opinions, the ability to appropriately structure the written response to meet the objectives in a logical and cohesive manner, and the writer's skill in generating and expressing complex ideas and remaining on topic.

- Coherence and cohesion: The overall clarity, cohesion, logical organization, sequencing, and linking of ideas and language for fluid and sensible readability.

- Lexical resource: The breadth, precision, and accuracy of word choice and vocabulary used for the given assignment conditions

- Grammatical range and accuracy: The breadth, precision, and accuracy of grammatical choices and sentence structures used for the given assignment conditions

The two sections below are called "Writing the Essay" and "Conventions of Standard English." The first section is designed to help you structure your essay and employ prewriting strategies that will help you brainstorm and begin writing the essay. The second section is common mistakes used in the English language. It also contains a section about American English spelling conventions. The IELTS™ accepts either British or American spelling. The information in this section should also inform the spelling of responses to the other sections of the exam. Lasting, there is information about interpreting graphs, which contains helpful tips for the first task on the Academic Test.

Writing the Essay

Brainstorming

One of the most important steps in writing an essay is prewriting. Before drafting an essay, it's helpful to think about the topic for a moment or two, in order to gain a more solid understanding of what the task is. Then, spending about five minutes jotting down the immediate ideas that could work for the essay is recommended. It is a way to get some words on the page and offer a reference for ideas when drafting. Scratch paper is provided for writers to use any prewriting techniques such as webbing, free writing, or listing. The goal is to get ideas out of the mind and onto the page.

Considering Opposing Viewpoints

In the planning stage, it's important to consider all aspects of the topic, including different viewpoints on the subject. There are more than two ways to look at a topic, and a strong argument considers those opposing viewpoints. Considering opposing viewpoints can help writers present a fair, balanced, and informed essay that shows consideration for all readers. This approach can also strengthen an argument by recognizing and potentially refuting the opposing viewpoint(s).

Drawing from personal experience may help to support ideas. For example, if the goal for writing is a personal narrative, then the story should be from the writer's own life. Many writers find it helpful to draw from personal experience, even in an essay that is not strictly narrative. Personal anecdotes or short stories can help to illustrate a point in other types of essays as well.

Moving from Brainstorming to Planning

Once the ideas are on the page, it's time to turn them into a solid plan for the essay. The best ideas from the brainstorming results can then be developed into a more formal outline. An outline typically has one main point (the thesis) and at least three sub-points that support the main point. Here's an example:

<u>Main Idea</u>
- Point #1
- Point #2
- Point #3

Of course, there will be details under each point, but this approach is the best for dealing with timed writing.

Staying On Track

Basing the essay on the outline aids in both organization and coherence. The goal is to ensure that there is enough time to develop each sub-point in the essay, roughly spending an equal amount of time on each idea. Keeping an eye on the time will help. If there are fifteen minutes left to draft the essay, then it makes sense to spend about 5 minutes on each of the ideas. Staying on task is critical to success, and timing out the parts of the essay can help writers avoid feeling overwhelmed.

Parts of the Essay

The *introduction* has to do a few important things:

- Establish the *topic* of the essay in original wording (i.e., not just repeating the prompt)
- Clarify the significance/importance of the topic or purpose for writing (not too many details, a brief overview)
- Offer a *thesis statement* that identifies the writer's own viewpoint on the topic (typically one-two brief sentences as a clear, concise explanation of the main point on the topic)

Body paragraphs reflect the ideas developed in the outline. Three-four points is probably sufficient for a short essay, and they should include the following:

- A *topic sentence* that identifies the sub-point (e.g., a reason why, a way how, a cause or effect)
- A detailed *explanation* of the point, explaining why the writer thinks this point is valid
- Illustrative *examples*, such as personal examples or real world examples, that support and validate the point (i.e., "prove" the point)
- A *concluding sentence* that connects the examples, reasoning, and analysis to the point being made

The *conclusion*, or final paragraph, should be brief and should reiterate the focus, clarifying why the discussion is significant or important. It is important to avoid adding specific details or new ideas to this paragraph. The purpose of the conclusion is to sum up what has been said to bring the discussion to a close.

Don't Panic!

Writing an essay can be overwhelming, and performance panic is a natural response. The outline serves as a basis for the writing and help writers keep focused. Getting stuck can also happen, and it's helpful to remember that brainstorming can be done at any time during the writing process. Following the steps of the writing process is the best defense against writer's block.

Timed essays can be particularly stressful, but assessors are trained to recognize the necessary planning and thinking for these timed efforts. Using the plan above and sticking to it helps with time management. Timing each part of the process helps writers stay on track. Sometimes writers try to cover too much in their essays. If time seems to be running out, this is an opportunity to determine whether all of the ideas in the outline are necessary. Three body paragraphs is sufficient, and more than that is probably too much to cover in a short essay.

More isn't always *better* in writing. A strong essay will be clear and concise. It will avoid unnecessary or repetitive details. It is better to have a concise, five-paragraph essay that makes a clear point, than a ten-paragraph essay that doesn't. The goal is to write one-two pages of quality writing. Paragraphs should also reflect balance; if the introduction goes to the bottom of the first page, the writing may be going off-track or be repetitive. It's best to fall into the one-two page range, but a complete, well-developed essay is the ultimate goal.

The Final Steps

Leaving a few minutes at the end to revise and proofread offers an opportunity for writers to polish things up. Putting one's self in the reader's shoes and focusing on what the essay actually says helps writers identify problems—it's a movement from the mindset of writer to the mindset of editor. The goal is to have a clean, clear copy of the essay. The following areas should be considered when proofreading:

- Sentence fragments
- Awkward sentence structure
- Run-on sentences
- Incorrect word choice
- Grammatical agreement errors
- Spelling errors
- Punctuation errors
- Capitalization errors

The Short Overview

The essay may seem challenging, but following these steps can help writers focus:

- Take one-two minutes to think about the topic.
- Generate some ideas through brainstorming (three-four minutes).
- Organize ideas into a brief outline, selecting just three-four main points to cover in the essay (eventually the body paragraphs).
- Develop essay in parts:
- Introduction paragraph, with intro to topic and main points
- Viewpoint on the subject at the end of the introduction
- Body paragraphs, based on outline
- Each paragraph: makes a main point, explains the viewpoint, uses examples to support the point
- Brief conclusion highlighting the main points and closing
- Read over the essay (last five minutes).
- Look for any obvious errors, making sure that the writing makes sense.

Conventions of Standard English

Errors in Standard English Grammar, Usage, Syntax, and Mechanics

Sentence Fragments

A *complete sentence* requires a verb and a subject that expresses a complete thought. Sometimes, the subject is omitted in the case of the implied *you*, used in sentences that are the command or imperative form—e.g., "Look!" or "Give me that." It is understood that the subject of the command is *you*, the listener or reader, so it is possible to have a structure without an explicit subject. Without these elements, though, the sentence is incomplete—it is a *sentence fragment*. While sentence fragments often occur in conversational English or creative writing, they are generally not appropriate in academic writing. Sentence fragments often occur when dependent clauses are not joined to an independent clause:

> *Sentence fragment*: Because the airline overbooked the flight.

The sentence above is a dependent clause that does not express a complete thought. What happened as a result of this cause? With the addition of an independent clause, this now becomes a complete sentence:

> *Complete sentence*: Because the airline overbooked the flight, several passengers were unable to board.

Sentences fragments may also occur through improper use of conjunctions:

> I'm going to the Bahamas for spring break. And to New York City for New Year's Eve.

> While the first sentence above is a complete sentence, the second one is not because it is a prepositional phrase that lacks a subject [I] and a verb [am going]. Joining the two together with the coordinating conjunction forms one grammatically-correct sentence:

> I'm going to the Bahamas for spring break and to New York City for New Year's Eve.

Run-ons

A *run-on* is a sentence with too many independent clauses that are improperly connected to each other:

> This winter has been very cold some farmers have suffered damage to their crops.

The sentence above has two subject-verb combinations. The first is "this winter has been"; the second is "some farmers have suffered." However, they are simply stuck next to each other without any punctuation or conjunction. Therefore, the sentence is a run-on.

Another type of run-on occurs when writers use inappropriate punctuation:

> This winter has been very cold, some farmers have suffered damage to their crops.

Though a comma has been added, this sentence is still not correct. When a comma alone is used to join two independent clauses, it is known as a **comma splice**. Without an appropriate conjunction, a comma cannot join two independent clauses by itself.

Run-on sentences can be corrected by either dividing the independent clauses into two or more separate sentences or inserting appropriate conjunctions and/or punctuation. The run-on sentence can be amended by separating each subject-verb pair into its own sentence:

This winter has been very cold. Some farmers have suffered damage to their crops.

The run-on can also be fixed by adding a comma and conjunction to join the two independent clauses with each other:

This winter has been very cold, so some farmers have suffered damage to their crops.

Parallelism

Parallel structure occurs when phrases or clauses within a sentence contain the same structure. Parallelism increases readability and comprehensibility because it is easy to tell which sentence elements are paired with each other in meaning.

Jennifer enjoys cooking, knitting, and to spend time with her cat.

This sentence is not parallel because the items in the list appear in two different forms. Some are *gerunds*, which is the verb + ing: *cooking, knitting*. The other item uses the *infinitive* form, which is to + verb: *to spend*. To create parallelism, all items in the list may reflect the same form:

Jennifer enjoys cooking, knitting, and spending time with her cat.

All of the items in the list are now in gerund forms, so this sentence exhibits parallel structure. Here's another example:

The company is looking for employees who are responsible and with a lot of experience.

Again, the items that are listed in this sentence are not parallel. "Responsible" is an adjective, yet "with a lot of experience" is a prepositional phrase. The sentence elements do not utilize parallel parts of speech.

The company is looking for employees who are responsible and experienced.

"Responsible" and "experienced" are both adjectives, so this sentence now has parallel structure.

Dangling and Misplaced Modifiers

Modifiers enhance meaning by clarifying or giving greater detail about another part of a sentence. However, incorrectly-placed modifiers have the opposite effect and can cause confusion. A *misplaced modifier* is a modifier that is not located appropriately in relation to the word or phrase that it modifies:

Because he was one of the greatest thinkers of Renaissance Italy, John idolized Leonardo da Vinci.

In this sentence, the modifier is "because he was one of the greatest thinkers of Renaissance Italy," and the noun it is intended to modify is "Leonardo da Vinci." However, due to the placement of the modifier next to the subject, John, it seems as if the sentence is stating that John was a Renaissance genius, not Da Vinci.

John idolized Leonard da Vinci because he was one of the greatest thinkers of Renaissance Italy.

The modifier is now adjacent to the appropriate noun, clarifying which of the two men in this sentence is the greatest thinker.

Dangling modifiers modify a word or phrase that is not readily apparent in the sentence. That is, they "dangle" because they are not clearly attached to anything:

> After getting accepted to college, Amir's parents were proud.

The modifier here, "after getting accepted to college," should modify who got accepted. The noun immediately following the modifier is "Amir's parents"—but they are probably not the ones who are going to college.

> After getting accepted to college, Amir made his parents proud.

The subject of the sentence has been change to Amir himself, and now the subject and its modifier are appropriately matched.

Inconsistent Verb Tense

Verb tense reflects when an action occurred or a state existed. For example, the tense known as *simple present* expresses something that is happening right now or that happens regularly:

> She *works* in a hospital.

Present continuous tense expresses something in progress. It is formed by to be + verb + -ing.

> Sorry, I can't go out right now. I *am doing* my homework.

Past tense is used to describe events that previously occurred. However, in conversational English, speakers often use present tense or a mix of past and present tense when relating past events because it gives the narrative a sense of immediacy. In formal written English, though, consistency in verb tense is necessary to avoid reader confusion.

> I traveled to Europe last summer. As soon as I stepped off the plane, I feel like I'm in a movie! I'm surrounded by quaint cafes and impressive architecture.

The passage above abruptly switches from past tense—*traveled, stepped*—to present tense—*feel, am surrounded*.

> I *traveled* to Europe last summer. As soon as I *stepped* off the plane, I *felt* like I was in a movie! I *was surrounded* by quaint cafes and impressive architecture.

All verbs are in past tense, so this passage now has consistent verb tense.

Split Infinitives

The *infinitive form* of a verb consists of "to + base verb"—e.g., to walk, to sleep, to approve. A *split infinitive* occurs when another word, usually an adverb, is placed between *to* and the verb:

> I decided *to simply walk* to work to get more exercise every day.

The infinitive *to walk* is split by the adverb *simply*.

> It was a mistake *to hastily approve* the project before conducting further preliminary research.

The infinitive *to approve* is split by *hastily*.

Although some grammarians still advise against split infinitives, this syntactic structure is common in both spoken and written English and is widely accepted in standard usage.

<u>Subject-Verb Agreement</u>
In English, verbs must agree with the subject. The form of a verb may change depending on whether the subject is singular or plural, or whether it is first, second, or third person. For example, the verb *to be* has various forms:

> I <u>am</u> a student.

> You <u>are</u> a student.

> She <u>is</u> a student.

> We <u>are</u> students.

> They <u>are</u> students.

Errors occur when a verb does not agree with its subject. Sometimes, the error is readily apparent:

> We is hungry.

Is is not the appropriate form of *to be* when used with the third person plural *we*.

> We are hungry.

This sentence now has correct subject-verb agreement.

However, some cases are trickier, particularly when the subject consists of a lengthy noun phrase with many modifiers:

> Students who are hoping to accompany the anthropology department on its annual summer trip to Ecuador needs to sign up by March 31st.

The verb in this sentence is *needs*. However, its subject is not the noun adjacent to it—Ecuador. The subject is the noun at the beginning of the sentence—students. Because *students* is plural, *needs* is the incorrect verb form.

> *Students* who are hoping to accompany the anthropology department on its annual summer trip to Ecuador *need* to sign up by March 31st.

This sentence now uses correct agreement between *students* and *need*.

Another case to be aware of is a *collective noun*. A collective noun refers to a group of many things or people but can be singular in itself—e.g., family, committee, army, pair team, council, jury. Whether or not a collective noun uses a singular or plural verb depends on how the noun is being used. If the noun refers to the group performing a collective action as one unit, it should use a singular verb conjugation:

> The family is moving to a new neighborhood.

The whole family is moving together in unison, so the singular verb form *is* is appropriate here.

The committee has made its decision.

The verb *has* and the possessive pronoun *its* both reflect the word *committee* as a singular noun in the sentence above; however, when a collective noun refers to the group as individuals, it can take a plural verb:

The newlywed pair spend every moment together.

This sentence emphasizes the love between two people in a pair, so it can use the plural verb *spend*.

The council are all newly elected members.

The sentence refers to the council in terms of its individual members and uses the plural verb *are*.

Overall though, American English is more likely to pair a collective noun with a singular verb, while British English is more likely to pair a collective noun with a plural verb.

Spelling and Punctuation

Spelling might or might not be important to some, or maybe it just doesn't come naturally, but those who are willing to discover some new ideas and consider their benefits can learn to spell better and improve their writing. Misspellings reduce a writer's credibility and can create misunderstandings. Spell checkers built into word processors are not a substitute for accuracy. They are neither foolproof nor without error. In addition, a writer's misspelling of one word may also be a word. For example, a writer intending to spell *herd* might accidentally type *s* instead of *d* and unintentionally spell *hers*. Since *hers* is a word, it would not be marked as a misspelling by a spell checker. In short, use spell check, but don't rely on it.

Guidelines for Spelling

Saying and listening to a word serves as the beginning of knowing how to spell it. Keep these subsequent guidelines in mind, remembering there are often exceptions because the English language is replete with them.

Guideline #1: Syllables must have at least one vowel. In fact, every syllable in every English word has a vowel.

- dog
- *haystack*
- *answering*
- *abstentious*
- *simple*

Guideline #2: The long and short of it. When the vowel has a short vowel sound as in *mad* or *bed,* only the single vowel is needed. If the word has a long vowel sound, add another vowel, either alongside it or separated by a consonant: bed/*bead*; mad/*made.* When the second vowel is separated by two spaces—*madder*—it does not affect the first vowel's sound.

Guideline #3: Suffixes. Refer to the examples listed above.

Guideline #4: Which comes first; the *i* or the *e*? Remember the saying, "*I* before *e* except after *c* or when sounding as *a* as in *neighbor* or *weigh*." Keep in mind that these are only guidelines and that there are always exceptions to every rule.

Guideline #5: Vowels in the right order. Another helpful rhyme is, "When two vowels go walking, the first one does the talking." When two vowels are in a row, the first one often has a long vowel sound and the other is silent. An example is *team*.

If you have difficulty spelling words, determine a strategy to help. Work on spelling by playing word games like Scrabble or Words with Friends. Consider using phonics, which is sounding words out by slowly and surely stating each syllable. Try repeating and memorizing spellings as well as picturing words in your head. Try making up silly memory aids. See what works best.

Homophones

Homophones are two or more words that have no particular relationship to one another except their identical pronunciations. Homophones make spelling English words fun and challenging like these:

Common Homophones		
affect, effect	cell, sell	it's, its
allot, a lot	do, due, dew	knew, new
barbecue, barbeque	dual, duel	libel, liable
bite, byte	eminent, imminent	principal, principle
brake, break	flew, flu, flue	their, there, they're
capital, capitol	gauge, gage	to, too, two
cash, cache	holy, wholly	yoke, yolk

Irregular Plurals

Irregular plurals are words that aren't made plural the usual way.

- Most nouns are made plural by adding –*s* (book*s*, television*s*, skyscraper*s*).

- Most nouns ending in *ch, sh, s, x,* or *z* are made plural by adding –*es* (church*es*, marsh*es*).

- Most nouns ending in a vowel + *y* are made plural by adding –*s* (day*s*, toy*s*).

- Most nouns ending in a consonant + *y,* are made plural by the *-y* becoming *-ies* (baby becomes *babies*).

- Most nouns ending in an *o* are made plural by adding –*s* (piano*s*, photo*s*).

- Some nouns ending in an *o*, though, may be made plural by adding –*es* (example: potato*es*, volcano*es*), and, of note, there is no known rhyme or reason for this!

- Most nouns ending in an *f* or *fe* are made plural by the *-f* or *-fe* becoming *-ves*! (example: wolf becomes *wolves*).

- Some words function as both the singular and plural form of the word (fish, deer).

- Other exceptions include *man* becomes *men, mouse* becomes *mice, goose* becomes *geese,* and *foot* becomes *feet.*

Contractions

The basic rule for making *contractions* is one area of spelling that is pretty straightforward: combine the two words by inserting an apostrophe (') in the space where a letter is omitted. For example, to combine *you* and *are*, drop the *a* and put the apostrophe in its place: *you're.*

> he + is = he's
> you + all = y'all (informal but often misspelled)

Note that *it's*, when spelled with an apostrophe, is always the contraction for *it is*. The possessive form of the word is written without an apostrophe as *its.*

Correcting Misspelled Words

A good place to start looking at commonly misspelled words here is with the word *misspelled*. While it looks peculiar, look at it this way: *mis* (the prefix meaning *wrongly*) + *spelled* = *misspelled*.

Let's look at some commonly misspelled words.

Commonly Misspelled Words					
accept	benign	existence	jewelry	parallel	separate
acceptable	bicycle	experience	judgment	pastime	sergeant
accidentally	brief	extraordinary	library	permissible	similar
accommodate	business	familiar	license	perseverance	supersede
accompany	calendar	February	maintenance	personnel	surprise
acknowledgement	campaign	fiery	maneuver	persuade	symmetry
acquaintance	candidate	finally	mathematics	possess	temperature
acquire	category	forehead	mattress	precede	tragedy
address	cemetery	foreign	millennium	prevalent	transferred
aesthetic	changeable	foremost	miniature	privilege	truly
aisle	committee	forfeit	mischievous	pronunciation	usage
altogether	conceive	glamorous	misspell	protein	valuable
amateur	congratulations	government	mortgage	publicly	vengeance
apparent	courtesy	grateful	necessary	questionnaire	villain
appropriate	deceive	handkerchief	neither	recede	Wednesday
arctic	desperate	harass	nickel	receive	weird
asphalt	discipline	hygiene	niece	recommend	
associate	disappoint	hypocrisy	ninety	referral	
attendance	dissatisfied	ignorance	noticeable	relevant	
auxiliary	eligible	incredible	obedience	restaurant	
available	embarrass	intelligence	occasion	rhetoric	
balloon	especially	intercede	occurrence	rhythm	
believe	exaggerate	interest	omitted	schedule	
beneficial	exceed	irresistible	operate	sentence	

Capitalization

Here's a non-exhaustive list of things that should be capitalized.

- the first word of every sentence
- the first word of every line of poetry
- the first letter of proper nouns (World War II)
- holidays (Valentine's Day)
- days of the week and months of the year (Tuesday, March)
- the first word, last word, and all major words in the titles of books, movies, songs, and other creative works (*To Kill a Mockingbird,* note that *a* is lowercase since it's not a major word, but *to* is capitalized since it's the first word of the title.
- titles when preceding a proper noun (President Roberto Gonzales, Aunt Judy)

When simply using a word such as president or secretary, though, the word is not capitalized.

Officers of the new business must include a *president* and *treasurer*.

Seasons—spring, fall, etc.—are not capitalized.

North, *south*, *east*, and *west* are capitalized when referring to regions but are not when being used for directions. In general, if it's preceded by *the* it should be capitalized.

I'm from the South.
I drove south.

Ellipses

An *ellipsis* (…) consists of three handy little dots that can speak volumes on behalf of irrelevant material. Writers use them in place of a word(s), line, phrase, list contents, or paragraph that might just as easily have been omitted from a passage of writing. This can be done to save space or to focus only on the specifically relevant material.

Exercise is good for some unexpected reasons. Watkins writes, "Exercise has many benefits such as …reducing cancer risk."

In the example above, the ellipsis takes the place of the other benefits of exercise that are more expected.

The ellipsis may also be used to show a pause in sentence flow.

"I'm wondering…how this could happen," Dylan said in a soft voice.

Commas

A *comma* (,) is the punctuation mark that signifies a pause—breath—between parts of a sentence. It denotes a break of flow. As with so many aspects of writing structure, authors will benefit by reading their writing aloud or mouthing the words. This can be particularly helpful if one is uncertain about whether the comma is needed.

In a complex sentence—one that contains a subordinate (dependent) clause or clauses—separate the clauses with commas.

> I will not pay for the steak, *because I don't have that much money.*

First, see how the purpose of each comma usage is to designate an interruption in flow. Then, notice how the last clause is dependent because it requires the earlier independent clauses to make sense.

Use a comma on both sides of an interrupting phrase.

> I will pay for the ice cream, chocolate and vanilla, and then will eat it all myself.

The words forming the phrase in italics are nonessential (extra) information. To determine if a phrase is nonessential, try reading the sentence without the phrase and see if it's still coherent.

A comma is not necessary in this next sentence because no interruption—nonessential or extra information—has occurred. Read sentences aloud when uncertain.

I will pay for his chocolate and vanilla ice cream and then will eat it all myself.

If the nonessential phrase comes at the beginning of a sentence, a comma should only go at the end of the phrase. If the phrase comes at the end of a sentence, a comma should only go at the beginning of the phrase.

Other types of interruptions include the following:

- interjections: Oh no, I am not going.
- abbreviations: Barry Potter, M.D., specializes in heart disorders.
- direct addresses: Yes, Claudia, I am tired and going to bed.
- parenthetical phrases: His wife, lovely as she was, was not helpful.
- transitional phrases: Also, it is not possible.

The second comma in the following sentence is called an Oxford comma.

> I will pay for ice cream, syrup, and pop.

It is a comma used after the second-to-last item in a series of three or more items. It comes before the word *or* or *and*. Not everyone uses the Oxford comma; it is optional, but many believe it is needed. The comma functions as a tool to reduce confusion in writing. So, if omitting the Oxford comma would cause confusion, then it's best to include it.

Commas are used in math to mark the place of thousands in numerals, breaking them up so they are easier to read. Other uses for commas are in dates (*March 19, 2016*), letter greetings (*Dear Sally,*), and in between cities and states (*Louisville, KY*).

Semicolons

The *semicolon* (*;*) might be described as a heavy-handed comma. Take a look at these two examples:

> I will pay for the ice cream, but I will not pay for the steak.
> I will pay for the ice cream; I will not pay for the steak.

What's the difference? The first example has a comma and a conjunction separating the two independent clauses. The second example does not have a conjunction, but there are two independent clauses in the sentence. So something more than a comma is required. In this case, a semicolon is used.

Two independent clauses can only be joined in a sentence by either a comma and conjunction or a semicolon. If one of those tools is not used, the sentence will be a run-on. Remember that while the clauses are independent, they need to be closely related in order to be contained in one sentence.

Another use for the semicolon is to separate items in a list when the items themselves require commas.

> The family lived in Phoenix, Arizona; Oklahoma City, Oklahoma; and Raleigh, North Carolina.

Colons

Colons have many miscellaneous functions. Colons can be used to proceed further information or a list. In these cases, a colon should only follow an independent clause.

> Humans take in sensory information through five basic senses: sight, hearing, smell, touch, and taste.

The meal includes the following components:

- Caesar salad
- spaghetti
- garlic bread
- cake

The family got what they needed: a reliable vehicle.

While a comma is more common, a colon can also proceed a formal quotation.

> He said to the crowd: "Let's begin!"

The colon is used after the greeting in a formal letter.

> Dear Sir:
> To Whom It May Concern:

In the writing of time, the colon separates the minutes from the hour (*4:45 p.m.*). The colon can also be used to indicate a ratio between two numbers (*50:1*).

Hyphens

The *hyphen* (-) is a little hash mark that can be used to join words to show that they are linked.

Hyphenate two words that work together as a single adjective (a compound adjective).

> honey-covered biscuits

Some words always require hyphens, even if not serving as an adjective.

> merry-go-round

Hyphens always go after certain prefixes like *anti-* & *all-*.

Hyphens should also be used when the absence of the hyphen would cause a strange vowel combination (*semi-engineer*) or confusion. For example, *re-collect* should be used to describe something being gathered twice rather than being written as *recollect*, which means to remember.

Parentheses and Dashes

Parentheses are half-round brackets that look like this: ( ). They set off a word, phrase, or sentence that is a afterthought, explanation, or side note relevant to the surrounding text but not essential. A pair of commas is often used to set off this sort of information, but parentheses are generally used for information that would not fit well within a sentence or that the writer deems not important enough to be structurally part of the sentence.

> The picture of the heart (see above) shows the major parts you should memorize.
> Mount Everest is one of three mountains in the world that are over 28,000 feet high (K2 and Kanchenjunga are the other two).

See how the sentences above are complete without the parenthetical statements? In the first example, *see above* would not have fit well within the flow of the sentence. The second parenthetical statement could have been a separate sentence, but the writer deemed the information not pertinent to the topic.

The dash (—) is a mark longer than a hyphen used as a punctuation mark in sentences and to set apart a relevant thought. Even after plucking out the line separated by the dash marks, the sentence will be intact and make sense.

> Looking out the airplane window at the landmarks—Lake Clarke, Thompson Community College, and the bridge—she couldn't help but feel excited to be home.

The dashes use is similar to that of parentheses or a pair of commas. So, what's the difference? Many believe that using dashes makes the clause within them stand out while using parentheses is subtler. It's advised to not use dashes when commas could be used instead.

Quotation Marks

The uses of quotation marks were discussed under the category *Dialogue*. Other uses include:

- around titles of songs, short stories, essays, and chapter in books
- to emphasize a certain word
- to refer to a word as the word itself

> Example: What's the meaning of "indubitably"?

Apostrophes

This punctuation mark, the apostrophe (') is a versatile little mark. It has a few different functions:

- Quotes: Apostrophes are used when a second quote is needed within a quote.

- In my letter to my friend, I wrote, "The girl had to get a new purse, and guess what Mary did? She said, 'I'd like to go with you to the store.' I knew Mary would buy it for her."

- Contractions: Another use for an apostrophe in the quote above is a contraction. *I'd* is used for *I would.*

- Possession: An apostrophe followed by the letter *s* shows possession (*Mary's* purse). If the possessive word is plural, the apostrophe generally just follows the word.

- The trees' leaves are all over the ground.

Interpretation of Graphs

Data can be represented in many ways including picture graphs, bar graphs, line plots, and tally charts. It is important to be able to organize the data into categories that could be represented using one of these methods. Equally important is the ability to read these types of diagrams and interpret their meaning.

A *picture graph* is a diagram that shows pictorial representation of data being discussed. The symbols used can represent a certain number of objects. Notice how each fruit symbol in the following graph represents a count of two fruits. One drawback of picture graphs is that they can be less accurate if each symbol represents a large number. For example, if each banana symbol represented ten bananas, and students consumed 22 bananas, it may be challenging to draw and interpret two and one-fifth bananas as a frequency count of 22.

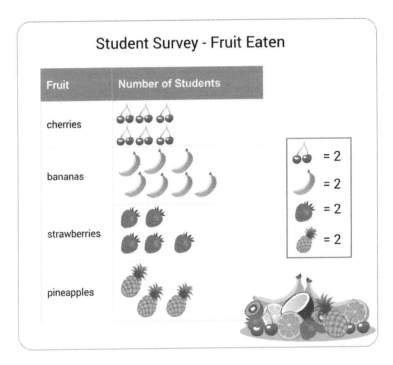

A *bar graph* is a diagram in which the quantity of items within a specific classification is represented by the height of a rectangle. Each type of classification is represented by a rectangle of equal width. Here is an example of a bar graph:

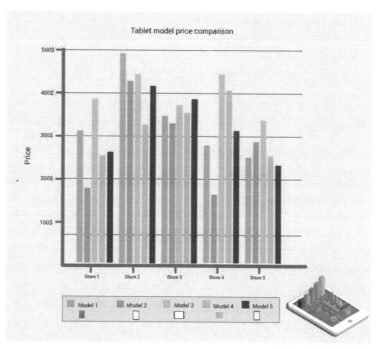

A *line plot* is a diagram that shows quantity of data along a number line. It is a quick way to record data in a structure similar to a bar graph without needing to do the required shading of a bar graph. Here is an example of a line plot:

A *tally chart* is a diagram in which tally marks are utilized to represent data. Tally marks are a means of showing a quantity of objects within a specific classification. Here is an example of a tally chart:

Number of days with rain	Number of weeks
0			
1	⌗
2	⌗
3	⌗
4	⌗ ⌗ ⌗ ||||
5	⌗	
6	⌗	
7					

Data is often recorded using fractions, such as half a mile, and understanding fractions is critical because of their popular use in real-world applications. Also, it is extremely important to label values with their units when using data. For example, regarding length, the number 2 is meaningless unless it is attached to a unit. Writing 2 cm shows that the number refers to the length of an object.

A circle graph, also called a pie chart, shows categorical data with each category representing a percentage of the whole data set. To make a circle graph, the percent of the data set for each category must be determined. To do so, the frequency of the category is divided by the total number of data points and converted to a percent. For example, if 80 people were asked what their favorite sport is and 20 responded basketball, basketball makes up 25% of the data ($\frac{20}{80}=.25=25\%$). Each category in a data set is represented by a *slice* of the circle proportionate to its percentage of the whole.

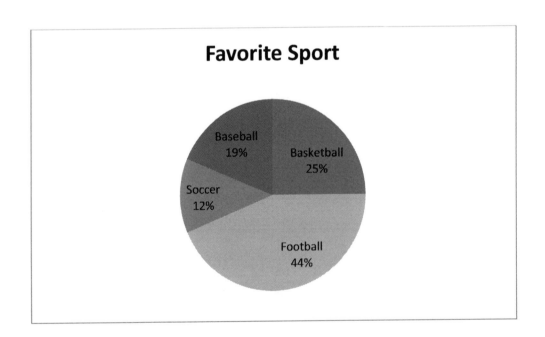

A scatter plot displays the relationship between two variables. Values for the independent variable, typically denoted by *x*, are paired with values for the dependent variable, typically denoted by *y*. Each set of corresponding values are written as an ordered pair (*x*, *y*). To construct the graph, a coordinate grid is labeled with the *x*-axis representing the independent variable and the *y*-axis representing the dependent variable. Each ordered pair is graphed.

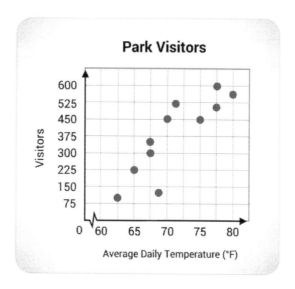

Like a scatter plot, a line graph compares two variables that change continuously, typically over time. Paired data values (ordered pair) are plotted on a coordinate grid with the *x*- and *y*-axis representing the two variables. A line is drawn from each point to the next, going from left to right. A double line graph simply displays two sets of data that contain values for the same two variables. The double line graph below displays the profit for given years (two variables) for Company A and Company B (two data sets).

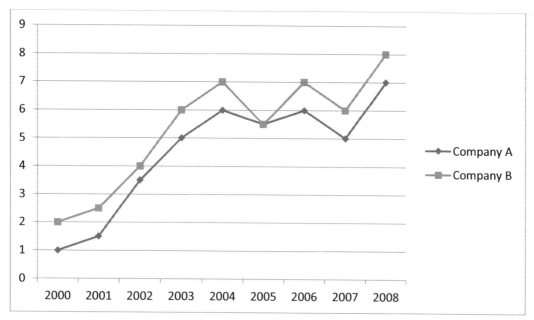

Choosing the appropriate graph to display a data set depends on what type of data is included in the set and what information must be shown. Histograms and box plots can be used for data sets consisting of individual values across a wide range. Examples include test scores and incomes. Histograms and box plots will indicate the center, spread, range, and outliers of a data set. A histogram will show the shape of the data set, while a box plot will divide the set into quartiles (25% increments), allowing for comparison between a given value and the entire set.

Scatter plots and line graphs can be used to display data consisting of two variables. Examples include height and weight, or distance and time. A correlation between the variables is determined by examining the points on the graph. Line graphs are used if each value for one variable pairs with a distinct value for the other variable. Line graphs show relationships between variables.

First Task

Academic Test

You should spend approximately 20 minutes on this task.

The graph below shows the percentage of calories from fast food among adults aged 20 and over, by age, race and ethnicity in United States from 2007–2010.

Summarize the main information presented in the graph and make any relevant comparisons.

Percentage of calories from fast food among adults aged 20 and over, by age and race and ethnicity: United States, 2007–2010

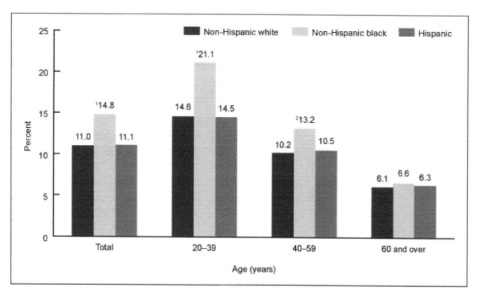

[1]Statistically different from non-Hispanic white and Hispanic adults ($p < 0.05$).
[2]Statistically different from non-Hispanic white adults ($p < 0.05$).
NOTE: Total estimates are age adjusted to the 2000 projected U.S. standard population using three age groups: 20–39, 40–59, and 60 and over.
SOURCE: National Health and Nutrition Examination Survey, 2007–2010.

Your response should be at least 150 words.

General Training Exam

You should spend approximately 20 minutes on this task.

You have lived in an apartment complex for two years. The manager recently sent letters to all tenants saying that monthly rental fees are increasing by $150 with all lease renewals to cover recent maintenance work and property upgrades. You disagree with this decision.

Prepare a letter of at least 150 words to the building manager. In your letter, cover the following:

- Briefly paraphrase the situation
- Explain specifically why you disagree with the rental increase
- Suggest alternative solutions

Address information is not to be included.

Begin your letter as follows:

To Whom It May Concern

Second Task

Academic Test

Prepare an essay of at least 250 words on the topic below.

In recent years, UK governmental agencies have been considering issues of national security and how it pertains to Internet usage. The government feels that a structured framework for surveillance to help protect the rights and privacy of UK citizens is necessary with the increased reliance on social media sites, ecommerce sites, and other Internet destinations.

Write an essay arguing whether you think government surveillance of the online-based activity and data collection of citizens should be lawful or not and what sorts of conditions or specific laws would be most effective. Use specific examples to support your argument.

General Training Exam

Prepare an essay of at least 250 words on the topic below.

Some people feel that sharing their lives on social media sites such as Facebook, Instagram, and Snapchat is fine. They share every aspect of their lives, including pictures of themselves and their families, what they ate for lunch, who they are dating, and when they are going on vacation. They even say that if it's not on social media, it didn't happen. Other people believe that sharing so much personal information is an invasion of privacy and could prove dangerous. They think sharing personal pictures and details invites predators, cyberbullying, and identity theft.

Write an essay to someone who is considering whether to participate in social media. Take a side on the issue and argue whether or not he/she should join a social media network. Use specific examples to support your argument.

Speaking

The IELTS™ Speaking Section assesses the test taker's ability to communicate effectively in English. This section lasts 11-14 minutes and consists of an oral interview between the test taker and an exam administrator and is recorded. The three parts to this test section are as follows:

- *Introduction and interview*: This section lasts 4-5 minutes and consists of general introductions between the test taker and the examiner. It will include basic questions about familiar life topics such as hobbies, family, studies, and home life. The questions are taken from a script to ensure equivalence in expectations for candidates.

- *Individual long turn*: Test takers will be handed a card that prompts them to talk about a specific topic, gives specific aspects that must be addressed, and instructs test takers to elaborate and more fully explain at least one of their points. This section lasts 3-4 minutes: one minute for preparation after reading the card, a one- to two-minute oral response, and then the examiner will ask the test taker one or two questions relating to the same topic. It should be noted that test takers are stopped after two minutes of talking, even if they have not addressed all of their points or the assignment's tasks, so test takers are encouraged to practice effective time management skills and use the one-minute preparation time to structure their speech and consider the time requirements. It is recommended that test takers jot down notes or a basic outline during the preparation period. Talking much less than 60-90 seconds will likely result in an incomplete answer and may detract from one's score. Some of the most effective and successful long turns result from the test takers drawing upon their own life experiences. The speech should be coherent, well-organized, grammatically correct, and compelling.

- *Discussion*: This section lasts 4-5 minutes and consists of more of a back-and-forth conversation between the test takers and examiner. The same topic addressed in Part 2 will be discussed, but this time, in more depth. The examiner is looking for evidence of the test taker's ability to analyze different viewpoints on issues and express and justify his or her opinion.

For all three tasks, examiners are evaluating test takers on the following four criteria:

- *Fluency and coherence*: The skill and ease with which the test taker talks with a steady, natural, and fluid rate, connecting ideas and words in a coherent and continuous manner. Test takers should structure their thoughts, points, and arguments in a logical sequence with appropriate use of cohesive devices like conjunctions, connecting words, and pronouns to link words, phrases, and sentences, and topics.

- *Lexical resource*: The breadth and precision of vocabulary used and the effectiveness of word choice to accurately and exactly convey intended meaning.

- *Grammatical range and accuracy*: The number and effect of grammatical errors, the length, complexity, and variety of the sentence structures delivered in the oral responses, the appropriate use of clauses, parts of speech, and language.

- *Pronunciation:* The proper pronunciation of the language used to answer the questions.

While this section can sound daunting, the good news is that the Speaking section of the IELTS™ is the easiest one to prepare for because the opportunities to practice are endless. Candidates should take advantage of every opportunity to practice their English speaking skills, not only to optimize their test performance, but also because they will be frequently conversing in English in diverse situations long after passing the exam. Nearly every situation presents a valid opportunity to practice—in the car, walking the dog, commuting to work, with a friend, doing errands, etc.

In addition to capitalizing on every chance to practice speaking, there are some other helpful strategies that successful test takers employ for this section.

Practice, but Don't Memorize

As mentioned, it's impossible to over-practice and the more speaking time a test taker has under his or her belt, the better. However, memorizing responses, particularly for the first two tasks (which tend to pose only a handful of possible questions), is not recommended. For one thing, scorers are looking for a natural speaking style that feels conversational and relaxed. Rehearsing and memorizing a predetermined response will likely lower one's delivery score even if the content is good. It is better to sound authentic and organic in the delivery of the answer, even if it means slightly less content is delivered in the allotted time. On that note, for the long turn, it's wise to practice speaking for two minutes to build confidence and time management skills for that task.

Listen and Read the Question Carefully

It's easy to jump to an answer when nervous, but successful test takers make sure to pay careful attention to the specific question posed in the task and ensure that their response addresses the exact points desired. For example, the first task usually asks general questions such as what do you enjoy doing in your spare time, what is your family like, or what are your favorite places to visit? Test takers who are overly rehearsed may begin to hear a familiar prompt and then assume they know what the question is asking and prepare to deliver their memorized response. However, this hastiness can lead to mistakes; oftentimes, there are slight changes in the wording of the questions such that the exact question test administrators are looking for is different than that assumed. Instead of what do you enjoy doing on your spare time, the question may be more specific and ask, what do you enjoy doing by yourself in your spare time? If a test taker did not listen carefully or jumped to a prepared answer about enjoying basketball with his or her team or shopping with friends, points would be deducted for inappropriate content for the intended answer.

Organize

Test takers should take advantage of the allotted preparation time to reflect on the question and organize their thoughts before they must deliver their response. Many people find it helpful to write down a couple of bullet points that they plan to highlight in their answer. These should be just a word or short phrase, rather than a whole sentence, so as to save time and sound organic and natural in the response. Reading fully composed sentences tends to sound overly rehearsed and may affect one's delivery score.

Speak clearly and simply

Many test takers feel anxious or self-conscious about delivering their responses with as little influence of an accent as possible. The good news is that the IELTS™ does not expect candidates to speak with any sort of "English" accent and scores are not influenced by the responder's accent one way or another as long as pronunciation is adequate. What is important is that the response is clear, audible, and comprehensible. After all, if scorers cannot hear or understand the recorded answer, they cannot award it with high marks. Test takers should speak as fluidly as possible, without rushing or interjecting long pauses or words of varying volumes. As much as possible, words should be enunciated with all syllables present and emphasizing those necessary for proper pronunciation. The more even and rhythmic the spoken answer, the better. One more point to note is that many test takers imagine that adding fancy vocabulary words will bolster their score. While demonstrating a rich vocabulary and strong command of English grammar and language skills is important, it is more important to ensure that words are used properly and that sentence structure and intended meaning are on point. If test takers are not confident in the meaning or proper usage of a word, it is better to use a seemingly simpler word whose meaning they are sure of.

Make speech flow

As mentioned, answers should flow as naturally and fluidly as possible. With that said, short pauses should be interjected at the end of each sentence or where commas would be used in written text to help listeners understand the thoughts and the organization of the response. Rushing into each subsequent sentence without an adequate pause tends to make answers sound confusing. To connect thoughts together and create a logical flow to the response, test takers should demonstrate command of the use of conjunctions. Employing effective connecting words and phrases such as: because, due to, for example, after this, if…then, and however.

Structure the answer

Although spoken language is often not as formal as written communication, answers should still be organized, with well-developed thoughts presented in a logical order. Successful test takers generate their ideas and plan their delivery during the reflection time prior to recording their responses. It is wise to start the answer by stating the topic thought (like a topic sentence in a written essay) and then expand or describe that thought in the subsequent sentences. Adding a concluding sentence that ties back to the beginning thought gives the listener clarity and pulls all the details together into a comprehensive and intelligent answer.

Tell a story

The most memorable conversations are those that include a captivating story. Speakers should try to make responses engaging and personal, when appropriate. This will not only make for a more enjoyable listening experience for scorers, but also can improve one's score by garnering more delivery points.

Be confident

Everyone has important things to say. Test takers should not worry about saying something "stupid" or "boring." They should speak from the heart and be confident in their command of English as well as their comprehension of the posed question. There is no need to rush when delivering the response; there is plenty of time in 45 seconds to get out a complete answer. On that note, if there is extra time at the end of the allotted recording time, it is generally recommended to simply end the response when the question has been fully answered rather than fill every last second with speaking. It is unnecessary to speak aimlessly at the end, as this can reduce one's content score if the answer starts deviating from what was asked. Test takers should just pace themselves; stay relaxed, and speak with authority.

Task 1

Let's talk about where you are from.

- Describe your favorite places in your city, town, or campus and explain why you like them.
- Do you think it's a good or bad place to live and why?
- What types of industries or jobs are popular in your town?

Now let's talk about your education and career plans.

- What would you like to study in university and why?
- What are your career goals and how will your studies help you reach these goals?
- What sorts of jobs have you had before?
- Do you prefer working or attending school? Why?

Task 2

Prompt card:

Some people think it's better to set realistic goals that they are confident they can achieve, while others argue it's better to set ambitious goals that one may fail to achieve.

What is your opinion?

Explain why.

> Preparation Time: 1 minute
> Response Time: 1-2 minutes

Rounding off questions:

Do you engage in any goal setting practices? Why or why not?

Task 3

Let's consider General Education requirements at universities.

- Do you think students attending university should have to take a variety of General Education courses in addition to the requirements of their major? Explain why or why not.

- What are the benefits and drawbacks of general education requirements for students?

- What courses do you think should be required of all university graduates, regardless of their major?

Now let's talk about textbooks.

- An increasing number of universities are now offering students the option to rent course textbooks instead of buy them. Which do you think is a better option?

- What are the benefits and drawbacks of each option?

- Do you or would you rent or buy your books?

Sample Answers

Task 1

Examiner: Let's talk about where you are from. Describe your favorite places in your city, town, or campus and explain why you like them.

Test taker: I live in New York City and I love it here. There are a lot of interesting places and constant action around you to watch and engage in if you so choose. General Grant's tomb is situated next to Riverside Park and has beautiful views of the Hudson river and George Washington Bridge. The architecture of the tomb and the bridge are striking and it is very lovely walking along the pathways. There is an interesting museum dedicated to the history of General Grant and New York City there as well. I also love the Natural History Museum, which is on the west side of Central Park. Although this museum does attract a lot of tourists, it does rightfully so because it has fascinating collections of rocks, minerals, historic natural specimens, and exhibits about animals, biomes, and the evolution of different cultures and societies. I saw a fantastic exhibit about the biodiversity and ecology of Cuba and saw an interesting planetarium show about the night sky. Besides the inherent wonder and intrigue of these places, I also enjoy these sites I have referenced because they are less well-known. This means they attract fewer tourists and are less crowded, while still embodying the energy and excitement of the city.

Examiner: Do you think it's a good or bad place to live and why?

Test taker: I think New York City is a great place to live because there is always so much going on so the opportunities are virtually endless. In my opinion, kids that grow up in the city are very worldly and mature because they are exposed to all sorts of people of diverse backgrounds and also have to learn to be responsible and independent at a younger age. Riding the subway and navigating through various neighborhoods teaches kids to be alert, organized, and instills good time management and judgment skills. In many cases, I think kids also learn about themselves and their interests well here because of the array of activities at their fingertips to sample and try out.

Examiner: What types of industries or jobs are popular in your town?

Test taker: There are nearly as many popular industries here as there are people. There's a market for most jobs. Business, finance, healthcare, fitness, fashion, architecture, science and research...pretty much all industries are equally viable career options. That's one of the many great benefits of living in such a large and thriving metropolis.

Examiner: Now let's talk about your education and career plans. What would you like to study in university and why?

Test taker: I would like to study business at university and also minor in marketing. In fact, I would like to get my MBA in business. I have always enjoyed entrepreneurship and so I think business is a great field. It also seems like a degree with versatile career options, and there will always be a need for people with business acumen, so it gives me confidence in job security. I can say the same things about marketing, and I enjoy thinking about advertisements and what drives people's buying decisions.

Examiner: What are your career goals and how will your studies help you reach these goals?

Test taker: If my education plans work out, I see myself owning my own small financial consulting company with a handful of employees under my supervision. With my marketing and business education, I will be able to make an educated business plan, drive customers to use the services at my firm, and build a business that generates significant revenue in an ethical way. I also hope that after a few years, my consulting firm is thriving, so I can pay off my student loan debt and buy a nice house.

Examiner: What sorts of jobs have you had before?

Test taker: I have worked at my mom's real estate firm since I was in Intermediate School. I mostly help with administrative tasks like calling clients, setting up showings, and organizing files. It is not particularly engaging work, but it is nice to see my mom and feel like I am helping her around the office. Also, because I have been assisting there for quite a few years at this point, I feel competent and comfortable there, which gives me confidence and makes me feel like I have a purpose. It's been rewarding to watch and play a part in the growth of the business over the past several years.

Examiner: Do you prefer working or attending school? Why?

Test taker: I actually prefer taking classes and attending school. I know this doesn't necessarily bode well for my future because we definitely work far more years of our life than we attend school. With that said, I've only ever had the administrative job at the real estate company. I anticipate enjoying my job more when I'm actually engaging in a vocation that I'm passionate about and running my own company.

Task 2

Examiner: Here is your prompt care. You have one minute to review it and then you have one to two minutes to respond. Don't worry about the need to keep time. I will alert you when the time is up.

Test taker: Okay.

Examiner: Okay. It is now time to begin speaking.

Test taker: I think it is better to set ambitious goals even if there is a chance of failure. When people set goals that are too easy, they are denying themselves the chance to really push themselves and grow. If someone doesn't set their sights high and just stays within their comfort zone, they'll never know what they can achieve and they might limit their potential. If instead, they set a big, lofty goal, they may fall short and not fully achieve it but they will likely still exceed where they would have landed with a low-level goal. For example, if an athlete wants to run a 5k race and get a fast time, she will be motivated to train really hard and stay disciplined if she sets a big goal that excites her. If she sets an easy goal that she is pretty confident she can achieve without putting in much work, she will probably not push herself as hard in workouts and might get a slower time.

Examiner: Thank you. Do you engage in any goal setting practices? Why or why not?

Test taker: I love setting goals and I regularly use goal setting as a technique to keep me organized, motivated, and efficient with my time. I set short- and long-term goals in many facets of my life including my studies, career, physical health, and financial wellness. Over time, I have found that I achieve more and feel more prepared and poised for success when I dedicate time and thought toward setting goals.

Task 3

Examiner: Let's consider General Education requirements at universities. Do you think students attending university should have to take a variety of General Education courses in addition to the requirements of their major? Explain why or why not.

I think it's a good idea when universities require that all of their students take a handful of classes distributed across all major academic disciplines in addition to the specific course requirements dictated by their major. This design exposes students to a variety of fields in the social and physical sciences, the arts, and mathematics so that all of that university's graduates have a well-rounded liberal arts education in addition to the advanced studies in their field of choice. This will help situate them well for a variety of careers and remain competitive and prepared for different types of jobs in case the economy changes or suffers and does not support their first choice.

Examiner: What are the benefits and drawbacks of general education requirements for students?

Test taker: Well, in addition to the benefits I mentioned, some students entering university haven't fully decided what they want to major in, so the general education requirements expose them to all sorts of topics and departments, so they can think about different careers, maybe even ones they didn't consider or know about. General education requirements encourage these students to dabble in different fields, which can help them find a good fit. A frequently-cited drawback of general education courses is that they are a waste of time and not engaging for students who enter university confident in their education and career goals. For example, if someone is certain that she wants to be a dentist, having to take a history course will likely feel extraneous and useless. Another drawback of programs that require too many general education courses is that each additional course mandated by the university equates to fewer courses possible in one's major, simply because of the conflict of time and scheduling demands. This can mean that students get less experience in their field of choice and do not have the opportunity to explore the finer details and advanced studies pertaining to their interests. All of this could ultimately hinder their career success or admissions opportunities for graduate programs.

Examiner: What courses do you think should be required of all university graduates, regardless of their major?

Test taker: Even though it can be argued that General Education requirements are a waste for students who know what they want to study, I do think that all students should take at least one or two academic writing courses regardless of their major. The ability to communicate effectively in an academic tone is paramount to students' future career success in virtually any field, even science and medicine. Imagine if a doctor conducts important research that will help patients improve their health. If that physician is unable to communicate it effectively and professionally in writing, his or her research won't be published and the patients won't benefit from the work.

Examiner: Now let's talk about textbooks. An increasing number of universities are now offering students the option to rent course textbooks digitally instead of buy them. Which do you think is a better option?

Test taker: I actually think it's financially prudent and wise overall to actually combine both practices: renting some digital textbooks and purchasing some traditional textbooks at the bookstore. I think it's smart to buy physical textbooks for those classes that one is taking in his or her major and rent digital books for required general education classes outside of one's major. That way, the student can save some money by buying fewer physical books with the cheaper e-textbooks, but will have the hard copy books for classes in his or her major in case the student wants to look back on them in future classes. With physical textbooks, students can highlight the material while they are reading to make sure they are really understanding the material as they study, which is very important for classes in his major.

Examiner: What are the benefits and drawbacks of each option?

Renting digital textbooks is a much less expensive option than the bookstore books and they obviously don't have the weight and bulk of real books. There also is an environmental benefit to consider: digital books reduce the number of trees that need to be cut down as well as all of the energy required to make physical textbooks in a publishing factory. Wood is a non-renewable resource and we virtually have an energy crisis on our hands, so any efforts—even seemingly minor—to reduce deforestation and energy footprint is a good thing. On the other hand, they are not easy to highlight or flag for review while studying and, if they are rented instead of purchased, once the course is over, the student no longer has access to the book for future reference. The benefits and drawbacks of physical textbooks are essentially the opposite. They are more expensive, bulky and heavy, and not as environmentally-friendly, yet they permit students to study and review their material with greater ease.

Examiner: Do you or would you rent or buy your books?

Test taker: So far, none of my courses have offered digital textbooks to rent so I have purchased paper books. I generally try to get them used to save money and reduce my environmental impact. Books for courses that are outside of my major or ones that I otherwise plan on never needing again, I try to resell after the course to recoup my costs.

FREE Test Taking Tips DVD Offer

To help us better serve you, we have developed a Test Taking Tips DVD that we would like to give you for FREE. **This DVD covers world-class test taking tips that you can use to be even more successful when you are taking your test.**

All that we ask is that you email us your feedback about your study guide. Please let us know what you thought about it – whether that is good, bad or indifferent.

To get your **FREE Test Taking Tips DVD**, email freedvd@studyguideteam.com with "FREE DVD" in the subject line and the following information in the body of the email:

- a. The title of your study guide.

- b. Your product rating on a scale of 1-5, with 5 being the highest rating.

- c. Your feedback about the study guide. What did you think of it?

- d. Your full name and shipping address to send your free DVD.

If you have any questions or concerns, please don't hesitate to contact us at freedvd@studyguideteam.com.

Thanks again!

Made in the USA
San Bernardino, CA
04 January 2018